P9-AQT-632

1. Cove of Wonders

FATIMA
Cove of Wonders

FATIMA
Cove of Wonders

by
Alphonse M. Cappa, S.S.P.

Translated by William H. Lyden

ST. PAUL EDITIONS

Imprimatur:
+Humberto Cardinal Medeiros
Archbishop of Boston

S. Bulfamante: cover photo

This edition was edited by the Daughters of St. Paul

Addresses of Pope John Paul II are reprinted with permission from
L'Osservatore Romano (English edition).

All rights reserved
to the Pious Society of St. Paul, for the Apostolate of the Press

Printed in the U.S.A., by the Daughters of St. Paul
50 St. Paul's Ave., Boston, MA 02130

The Daughters of St. Paul are an international congregation of women religious serving the Church with the communications media.

DEDICATION

To those who teach souls to love our heavenly Mother more and to seek her intercession with greater fervor.

Contents

PREFACE

Books on Fatima are increasing in number, month after month. It is a sign that Fatima's story is enticing to those who write and to those who read.

Fatima is a voice—mighty, impelling—from heaven! The voice of our Mother! Fatima has secrets for every heart; promises to give to all—secrets and promises which were confided to three innocent souls and which have in themselves the persuasion and the strength to conquer and transform the world.

You must know these secrets, share these hidden treasures and assure such promises for yourself.

For this simple reason this book exists.

—The Author

ACKNOWLEDGMENT

Four important documents were issued by the living witness of the apparitions of Our Lady of Fatima, Lucia Dos Santos, now Sister Maria-Lucia Das Dores, under the express command of the Most Reverend Bishop of Leiria (Portugal), whom the Portuguese people like to call "the Bishop of Our Lady of Fatima."

The first document is a very precious *Contribution to the Biography of Little Jacinta*, written by Lucia with great love and affection "to the most intimate friend of her childhood," of whom she said: "I am indebted in great part to her companionship for the preservation of my innocence." In this document Lucia textually writes: "For all these anecdotes (which she narrated) and for many others, I keep her in great esteem of holiness.... And I hope that God shall grant her the halo of sanctity, for the glory of the most Blessed Virgin."

The second document relates *The Intimate Story of Fatima, as It Really Is:* the true character, the intimate nature, the spirit of the devotion to our Lady.

These two documents, written before the year 1938 on more than eighty typewritten sheets, were followed by two other documents, written in the year 1941, on about sixty typewritten folios, after the Bishop of Leiria commanded her again to put in writing *"Other Things That She Could Remember About the Two Little Children, Francisco and Jacinta,* and *An Exact Narration of the Apparitions, Without Concealing Anything of What Was Actually Revealed."*

It was a very great sacrifice for Sister Maria-Lucia to put on paper so many striking revelations and secrets. Indeed, a true martyrdom for her modesty. Forwarding the manuscript to the Bishop, she wrote: "I believe I have now written everything that Your Excellency has commanded me to write. Until the present time it has been possible for me to keep hidden in my soul most of the intimate secrets connected with the apparitions in the Cova da Iria. When I was obliged to speak of them, I sought to touch upon them as lightly as possible, so as not to reveal what I hold most sacred. But now that I am bound by obedience...here are the facts!... I return what does

14

not belong to me!..." then, as if crushed by this violation of the silence of the cloister, which she considered "a great grace," she continues: "And I remain like a skeleton, stripped of everything, even of my very life, and hung up in a museum, to the gaze of visitors, as a monument of the misery and the futility of what passes away. So stripped of everything, I will remain in the museum of the world, reminding the passers-by not of the misery and the nothingness, but of the greatness of the divine mercies" (*Letter to the Bishop of Leiria*, Dec. 8, 1941).

A Portuguese priest the Rev. Luigi Gonzaga Da Fonseca, S.J., Professor of the Pontifical Institute in Rome, through the gentle benevolence of the Bishop of Leiria, succeeded in securing these four and many other documents concerning the wonders of Fatima, and published a most complete story about Fatima, under the title *"Le Meraviglie di Fatima"*; a book read, corrected and annotated by Sister Maria-Lucia herself and edited with many editions, each one amplified with more abundant documentations, more news about persons, places and circumstances, and translated into many languages.

Whoever finds himself constrained—as it happened to me—to follow the account of Fatima in accordance with the work of the Rev. Da Fonseca, feels the need to draw from his fountain of facts. This I did: and this I frankly declare, certain that the distinguished author will not be displeased that even I should have expressed my homage to our Blessed Mother, the consolation and salvation of us all.

Other sources of information in this volume are the following books, and grateful acknowledgment is hereby made to their authors:

As Grandes Maravilhas de Fatima, by Visconde De Montelo.

Fatima: Gracas, Segredos, Misterios, by Antero De Figneiredo.

Fatima, das Portugiesische Lourdes, by Dr. Ludwig Fischer.

Fatima im Lichte der Kirchlichen Auktoritaet, by Dr. Ludwig Fischer.

Trois Favoris de la Vierge, by Myriam De G.

Fatima, by Icilio Felici.

La Madonna di Fatima, by Luigi Moresco.
Gli Occhi Che Videro la Madonna, by Luigi Moresco.

I wish also to thank the translator, William H. Lyden, for his very kind help. And may he and I have the freedom to say as Sister Maria-Lucia says: "May the good God and the Immaculate Heart of Mary deign to accept the poor sacrifices they asked for, to revive in the heart of man the spirit of faith, confidence and love."

—The Author

PART ONE

Preparation Through Prayer and Sacrifice

The Village of Fatima

At the beginning of the twentieth century, Fatima, a small village in Portugal, was virtually unknown to the world beyond its own boundary. It simply had no significance whatever for the outside world. It did not appear even on the maps used by the Portuguese public. Situated on the side of a minor mountain range called the *Serra de Aire*, it drowsed away its years peacefully, humbly, untrod by any strangers, and unsung by the rest of humanity. Its very name is a legend pointing back to ancient Moorish domination.

But today that is all changed. Today Fatima knows no boundaries. The whole world kneels at its doorstep. Its fame and glory are published in almost every language. Why this sudden change? Because there in 1917, Mary, the Immaculate, the Queen of Heaven, came down personally in celestial apparitions to this impoverished hamlet to converse with human beings, chaste and chosen souls, in words of affection, sympathy, exhortation, promise—yes, and even of warning. But she came principally as a messenger of peace and love.

Fatima is but a minor parish belonging, since 1920, to the very poor Diocese of Leiria, and situated almost in the center of Portugal, about seventy-five miles north of Lisbon, in the province of Estremadura.

Of all the provinces of Portugal, this one presents the most outstanding topography. The landscape is very irregular. Every aspect of this region has its own peculiar characteristics, which have notably influenced the temperament and customs of the inhabitants.

To one traveling northward from Lisbon, the panorama unfolds a continual change of hue and tints of green as far as Alcobaca. Farther ahead blossoms the beautiful valley of Batalha and Leiria. On the immediate road to Fatima, however, the scenery changes abruptly to the very opposite and loses all its charms. The land becomes rough, more and more arid and colorless.

Presently there looms in view the Serra da Aire. A dismal scene, the soil is parched and unproductive. Stray flocks of sheep may be seen on the mountainside, which is bare of vegetation except for some scattered shrubs and thin clusters of oak and olive trees along the ridges that help to relieve the depressing monotony of the terrain. On a slope of the mountain, high up in the Serra, nestled in an atmosphere of deep loneliness and almost complete abandonment, is the little village called *Fatima*.

Just beyond this is the famous *Cova da Iria*, so called because of its contour, a desolate, dry and stony basin, not unlike an amphitheater, and measuring about a third of a mile in diameter.

Here in this Cove, devoid of every natural attraction, we have the very scene of those celestial visitations about which this book is concerned—the spot hallowed by the presence of the Queen of Heaven and selected by divine Providence to radiate love and benediction to the far corners of the earth in return for grateful, filial devotion to Mary, the Immaculate.

If we could tarry awhile with the mountain-folk of the Aire, we should soon observe the striking peculiarities of their nature and surroundings. These people speak little; consequently, their disposition seems cold and heartless. But their whole life centers around three great loves: God, the family, and manual labor.

Their houses are small and crude, with low, narrow windows. The kitchen contains nothing but a wooden table, a closet for the utensils, and a fireplace. The living room might boast of a rustic table with the inevitable crucifix on it. Holy images are pasted on the walls or fastened with rusty nails. The bedrooms are poor and bare, except for the cot. Outside, and adjoining the house, is the sheep-fold, with perhaps a fig or olive tree or a few oaks growing close by.

The mountaineer's life is hard and laborious. He wrests a meager sustenance from his toil on the mountains or in the fields. His clothing is generally of the poorest type. On exceptional occasions and feast days he wears a tight cap, a short embroidered jacket, and trousers that are somewhat tight at the waist and fall wide to the ankles.

The women have charge of their proper domain—the home. They prepare the meals, spin, weave, carry out the household chores, and watch carefully over the spiritual and physical growth of the children. They are fond of wearing their hair parted down through the middle, occasionally with a headdress of a tight hat, and a long kerchief under it falling gracefully to the shoulders. For additional ornamentation they prefer earrings, and for special festivities, gold chains to hang around the neck.

To the children falls the work of tending the sheep. They leave the house early in the morning, taking their lunches along with them, and do not return until sunset when the Angelus rings out for them the close of the day and summons all to prayer. Few of them ever learn to read or write. Their only schooling consists of elementary knowledge and religious truths and domestic skills imparted by the mother of the house.

Only for a short time in the evening, after supper and the strenuous labors of the day, do all enjoy the intimacy of family life, for they must retire early to gain the proper rest and to be refreshed for their daily toil. It is a general custom, before retiring, for the whole family to join in reciting the rosary, the father leading slowly and reverently while the mother and children make the responses with equal fervor and devotion. Then follow the prayers invoking God's blessing upon their repose, and finally the "De Profundis." It was this environment, this constant devotion, this purity and simplicity of life that drew down from on high the tender affections of Mary, the Queen of the Most Holy Rosary.

This tiny speck of earth, this insignificant portion of Portugal, was set apart in the inscrutable ways of divine Wisdom and chosen, like Israel of old, to help as a mighty instrument to further God's redemption and sanctification of the world through Mary, His Mother, the Immaculate Conception.

"The Queen of Heaven," stated Cardinal Emanuel Goncalves Cerejeira, Patriarch of Lisbon in 1931, "descended upon the land that was her possession from the beginning, a land consecrated to her with the birth of the nation and given the name *Terra de Santa Maria*, the 'Land of Our Lady.' "

The Mother of God willed to show herself to this duty-loving people with exceptional maternal tenderness. She desired to place them in her powerful protection. She is ever solicitous for those who never tired of honoring her in the beautiful prayer of the rosary.

She determined to establish her very throne at Fatima, in the territory that had belonged to her for centuries. From that glorious throne she willed to send out a universal message: that not only Portugal but all nations were to be dedicated to her; that she would listen to the cries of a repentant and strife-weary world and grant peace to warring nations—a great and enduring peace after the castigations visited upon man for his hardness of heart.

She warned, however, of greater calamities to befall the world if mankind continued to precipitate itself into more degrading sensuality, and of the terrible fate of those sinners who would merit punishment at the hands of the eternal Judge.

In fine, she came to tell the world that her loving and immaculate heart is ever a sure refuge for souls torn by tribulation and sorrow, and that she would never fail to assist those who sought her aid under the titles of "Our Lady of Fatima," the "Immaculate Heart of Mary," and the "Queen of the Most Holy Rosary."

The wonderful story of Fatima has been prepared and composed for your inspiration and spiritual profit by a young priest, whose sole reward is the consciousness of his humble instrumentality in spreading the fame and glory of our heavenly Mother.

Typical Mountain Children

"The foolish things of the world has God chosen to put to shame the wise; and the weak things of the world has he chosen to confound the strong; and the base things of the world and the despised has God chosen, and the things that are not, to overcome the things that are, lest any flesh should pride itself before him" (1 Cor. 1:27-28).

History has often confirmed these words of St. Paul. For the evangelization of the world, did not the Master choose twelve lowly, uncouth, unlettered fishermen? Were not the earliest Christian communities composed of the very poor, even of slaves? The wealthy, the great, the doctors, the orators, the philosophers and theologians were to come later when the "folly" of the cross had conquered the best intellects and established itself as the only true wisdom.

Pope Gregory VII, saint and great champion of the liberty of the Church, was the son of poor peasants. St. Joan of Arc, the heroic martyr, with the standard of the cross in one hand and the sword of justice in the other, liberated her beloved country from its enemies, yet she was a poor, illiterate shepherdess, directed by heavenly "voices." Bernadette Soubirous, the chosen seer of Lourdes, was born of the lowliest parentage. Pope Pius X, Giuseppe Sarto, the Pope of the Blessed Eucharist now one of God's saints, rose from the humblest family to fill the greatest office on earth.

Fatima, too, had its seers and its unassuming background of poverty that was to emerge into a splendor of achievement and reputation that could have no other direction than that of the divine Ruler of the universe.

But who were these children, these historic persons, these elected souls chosen by the divine Artist to become the earthly actors in a spectacle that was to captivate the interest and the affection of the whole Christian world?

They were three innocent little shepherd children, tending the sheep of their parents. The eldest, only ten years of age, was named Lucia Dos Santos; the others, her cousins, were Francisco Marto, nine years of age, and his sister Jacinta, aged seven. All three were natives of Aljustrel, a dependency of Fatima and situated on its border.

They were typical mountain children—healthy, robust, and rugged from daily exposure to the elements, timid and slightly awkward in their speech and movements, as might be expected from their total lack of social contacts. They could neither read nor write, and, considering their circumstances, they had no desire for such education. But their fresh little minds and souls were filled with elementary religious and moral truths taught to them by their conscientious parents, especially their mothers. Of the three, only Lucia had made her First Holy Communion—an uncommon privilege for ten-year-olds in those parts.

The youngest of six children in the family of Anthony and Mary-Rose Dos Santos, Lucia was born on March 22, 1907. From the tender age of eight, her principal occupation had been that of shepherdess, watching over a small flock of sheep pastured in the neighboring mountains.

Francisco and Jacinta were the two youngest members of the family of Peter and Olympia Marto, who were blessed by God with eleven children. Francisco was born on June 11, 1908; Jacinta on March 11, 1910. They had not yet reached an age where they could be trusted alone with the care of the flocks, so they passed all their time at home, helping their mother, playing, and learning to pray. But at times they were permitted to accompany their cousin Lucia and to assist her in the endless task of rounding up the stray lambs.

One evening, on their way home from the fields, Jacinta dropped back into the middle of the flock, took up one of the bleating little animals in her arms, and stood there rigidly, as in a pose.

"Jacinta, what are you doing there?" exclaimed Lucia.

"I am imitating Jesus," she responded with childish candor. "Remember that beautiful picture that was given to me for a present—Jesus with the sheep all around Him, and carrying one on His shoulders?"

These are the "little ones of the kingdom of God," who were to be privileged beyond many, and were destined to enjoy Mary's highest predilection.

Taught in nature's school, they saw God in the brilliance of the dawn and in the splendor of the sun at eventide; in the twinkling of the stars; in the pale light of the peaceful moon.

In the weary routine of tending the flocks the children naturally had to devise ways and means of entertaining themselves. They said their prayers over and over, even to the repetition of the rosary. They would raise their voices in loud, repeated shouts, to hear their words bound back to them in echoes from the surrounding cliffs. Jacinta noticed that the word "Mary" seemed to have the best echo of any, and she would repeat it over and over to their greatest delight.

When they tired of praying the set formulas of prayers learned at home, they invented their own way of saying them. Thus they would shorten the rosary: making the sign of the cross and holding the beads in their hands, they would begin by one saying the first two words and nothing more: "Hail Mary...." The others, likewise using only two words, would answer: "Holy Mary...." When they came to the large beads, they simply said in chorus, "Our Father..."—just the two words.

"That way," said Lucia, "we could pray the rosary in a jiffy."

This abbreviation of their prayers caused them no loss of tranquility, no qualms of conscience. They had done their duty, so they thought, and were soon lost again in play.

One morning in the year 1915, Lucia and three other girls from the village found themselves on the *Cabeco,* a small mountain fringed with olive trees, located near Aljustrel, and extending towards Fatima.

They had just eaten their lunch and were beginning to say some prayers. Then, looking up, they saw a strange, luminous figure hovering over one of the olive trees. Its outline was that of a human being, but it resembled a statue of snowy crystal glittering in the noon day sun.

"Oh, look!" one exclaimed, "what can it be?"

Becoming thoroughly frightened, they began to speak to one another and to pray, while observing every movement of the vision.

Finally it disappeared, and they scampered home.

In the space of a few weeks they were startled by the unusual appearance two more times.

Conquered by some natural instinct, or, obedient to some supernatural inspiration (we do not know which), Lucia did not mention the incidents to her parents.

But the other three were more talkative. Childlike, they could not conceal their emotions nor hold their tongues, and soon their secret was out. The neighbors began to discuss it, and finally it reached the ears of Lucia's parents. Her mother scolded her for her imprudent silence and demanded to know what all this talk was about.

"Come, Lucia!" She was impatient now. "They say you saw something. What was it? Speak up!"

"I don't know, Mamma," she replied disconsolately.

Then the child described the apparition as best she could for her tender age. She explained that the outlines of the object were not distinct, because of the distance that separated them, but that it resembled a statue covered with a white sheet.

The mother shook her head angrily and said, "Nonsense! You are a simpleton!" And she would hear no more of it. Such childish fancies!

The Heavenly Messengers

The memory of these happenings of 1915 had almost vanished from the village of Aljustrel—except from those who loved to taunt Lucia occasionally about her "statue covered with a sheet" —when Lucia was again thrown into violent agitation by a fourth appearance of the phenomenon, but this time in a more satisfactory and impressive manner. It occurred one morning in the spring of 1916. We do not specify the exact date because Lucia, on account of her tender age, had not yet learned to count the days.

On this occasion Lucia was accompanied by her two cousins, Francisco and Jacinta, who, after many pleadings with their parents, had gained permission to go to the pasture, and from then on were to become Lucia's inseparable companions.

Early in the morning it began to rain. The children hastened to find shelter in a place well known to Lucia, a hollow enclosure, or grotto, beneath some jutting rocks on the side of the Mount Cabeco. Here they rested, ate their lunches, said the rosary together (both the long and the short ones, no doubt), and even tarried there after the weather had cleared, playing games and indulging in pleasant conversation.

Without any perceptible cause or warning signal, they felt the shock of a terrific, roaring wind. Irresistibly urged to abandon the cave, they ran to the opening to see the source of this sudden disturbance, only to be met with another more profoundly impressive. Just over the fringe of olive trees hovered the same mysterious figure that had appeared to Lucia three times before. But this time it moved towards the children closer and closer, still suspended in mid-air, its contour and lineaments growing gradually more and more distinct, until it finally came to rest immediately above them.

They recognized the features as being that of a youth of about fifteen, handsome beyond compare. Then he began to speak. In a voice immeasurably soft and tender, he told them not to be frightened. Banishing all fear from their trembling frames, he continued, "I am the Angel of peace. Pray with me!" With that, he changed to a kneeling posture, and bowed his head reverently towards the earth. The children imitated his action and repeated after him the following prayer:

"My God, I believe in You, I hope in You, I adore and love You. I ask pardon for all who do not believe, who do not hope in You, who do not adore nor love You."

This prayer was repeated three times at the gracious insistence of the heavenly visitor. Then he rose from his knees and addressed them again:

"Let that prayer be dear to you. The Sacred Hearts of Jesus and Mary will hear and be touched by the voice of your supplication."

In a moment he was gone, leaving the children filled with wonder and amazement.

Late in the summer of the same year, about noon on a hot, sultry day, while the elders enjoyed the "siesta," the children, who were relieved of their duties in the fields, were playing in the garden

behind Lucia's home. In a deep recess of the garden there was a spring covered with large flat stones and surrounded by shrubs and trees. The children often went there to play or to sit and talk and refresh themselves, drinking of the cool, pure water of the spring.

Playing and singing, their laughter mingled with the songs of the birds in the trees. Then, before their startled countenances, there appeared in the midst of them a beautiful, radiant figure, overpowering in majesty, and not unlike the angel that had come to the grotto and taught them how to pray.

"What are you doing now?" he said to them in a tone of ineffable kindness. And without waiting for an answer, he admonished them: "You must pray, and pray unceasingly. The most holy Hearts of Jesus and Mary have designs of great mercy for you. You are to offer up to the Lord unending prayers and sacrifices!"

"What does that mean—'to make sacrifices'?" Lucia ventured to ask, when she had partly recovered from her fright.

"Everything you do can be a sacrifice," replied the heavenly messenger, "and be offered up to our Lord as an act of reparation for sin, by which He is so grossly offended, and as a supplication for the conversion of sinners. Strive in this manner to merit God's compassion and blessing of peace for your beloved country. I am its guardian angel. I beseech you to accept, in humble submission, the trials that heaven is about to impose upon you."

God's holy designs for these children were rapidly taking shape now that they had received from the ambassador of the Most High an invitation to a novitiate of prayer in the mystical school of the angels. In the short space of a few months, these innocent souls had listened with ecstatic joy to the voices of two of the heavenly hierarchy. Their hearts and minds were instructed and uplifted and their souls suffused with divine grace. Soon they were to have the privilege of another celestial visit, a most happy and consoling one.

Ever since the day that the angel of peace had come to them in the cavern of the Cabeco and had taught them the beautiful prayer of faith, hope and charity, the place had become a holy shrine for them. There they went as often as they could to kneel on the holy ground and say the prescribed prayer over and over again, with ever-increasing delight. Wrapped in obedient love and devotion, they came to regard this prayer that had come from the lips of the angel of peace as a canticle of joy.

Neither did they omit their other prayers: the chaplet of their Blessed Mother, the prayer to their guardian angels, and now, in addition, those contained in their most recent order from the protecting spirit of peace.

The novitiate of prayer had begun for them in full earnest.

It was autumn. The little shepherds were once more on the Cabeco and had gone to the cavern to carry out their usual devotions. Lost in adoration and pleading with the divine Mercy to help their fatherland and to spare sinful humanity, they did not notice the cave filling with a strange, supernatural light. The children were unaware that they were not alone until a voice, musical and pleasing beyond any earthly harmony, fell on their ears and caused them to lift their eyes.

Before them stood the beautiful, transfigured form of a youth, arrayed in the splendor of a thousand suns. In one hand he held a golden chalice, in the other the sacred host, from which blood dripped into the holy vessel. In an instant he had stepped among them, leaving the chalice and sacred species suspended in mid-air in a halo of glory. Bowing his head to the ground, he requested them reverently to follow his action and to repeat after him:

"Oh Most Holy Trinity, Father, Son, and Holy Spirit, I adore You profoundly and offer the most precious body, blood, soul and divinity of our Lord and Savior, Jesus Christ, present in every tabernacle of the world, in reparation for all the outrages, sacrileges, and indifference of mankind, by which He is continually offended. And through the infinite merits of His Sacred Heart, and through the intercession of the Immaculate Heart of Mary, I plead for the conversion of unfortunate sinners."

Symbolic of the divine mystery they had just invoked, they offered this prayer of universal reparation three times.

The angel then ascended and took the host and chalice once more in his hands. The children still knelt in a transport of joy and adoration. The only sign of life within them was the violent throbbing of their hearts, the look of longing, of holy thirst and hunger in their blessed eyes, seeking, so to speak, a still more intimate, more complete and satisfying union with their eucharistic Lord.

Could it be possible? Would Jesus come so far and in this special way from His throne on high, and not, in His infinite tenderness and love for His three little friends, lavish the full benefits of His eucharistic presence upon them? Did He not say of children that unless we become as they, we cannot hope to enter His kingdom? And He so loved these three little ones that He brought His kingdom down to them! Smiling, the angel, the priestly dispenser, advanced and placed the miraculous host on Lucia's tongue. To Francisco and Jacinta he gave the most precious blood, to each a half to drink, saying, "Receive the body and blood of our Savior, Jesus Christ, so horribly outraged by ungrateful men. Make reparation for the sins of the world and for the consolation of your God!"

In wondrous joy and gratitude, and in the loving care of their guardian angels, the little communicants bowed their heads in lengthy adoration, repeating three times again the prayer of the angelic visitor.

Night was beginning to descend upon the Mount Cabeco when the happy little shepherds reluctantly left the grotto which was filled with the fragrance of heavenly incense in the wake of the vanished angel. Their parents were worried and could not imagine what should keep them so long in the fields. Dazed and stunned by the momentous happenings of the day, they succeeded with a few evasive answers in quieting the anxiety of their elders. With divine assistance, they kept their secrets well locked within their hearts. They had also preserved a prudent and probably inspired silence concerning the visions that preceded the one just described. In fact, we know this to be a certainty; it was learned twenty-five years later from the ecclesiastical authorities after the death of Francisco and Jacinta.

But the cumulative effect of these startling manifestations was beginning to be markedly evident in the behavior of the children. Later in life, Lucia was asked to describe the difference in effect, if any, between the apparitions of the angels and those of the Blessed Virgin at Fatima. Both, she affirmed, were accompanied by a feeling of great joy and peace of soul. Those of the Virgin were never frightening, but those of the angels, on the contrary, were invariably overpowering. The radiance of supernatural light and power left them totally unconscious of their surroundings. For days their senses were dulled, they showed less and less interest in the worldly life about them and suffered, in fact, an extreme bodily weariness. They had no desire for play or self-entertainment, and they rarely spoke.

But their souls were steeped in prayer and meditation, delighting in the memories of the favors and graces given them in the heavenly visitations. Eagerly and obediently they accepted every discomfort in a spirit of sacrifice. In addition to their other favorite devotions, they said the beautiful prayers prescribed by the angels.

But God did not send His holy ministers to depress them, but rather to enlighten and invigorate them, so that in a short time they reassumed their natural liveliness of mind and body, played and sang together, and performed all their duties in a natural manner.

It is to be understood that these illiterate, secluded, and inexperienced children did not as yet grasp the full meaning of the designs that Providence had for them. God's grace ordinarily comes by degrees, measured by the willing cooperation of the fortunate recipient. The children had already risen high on the mystical ladder that unites heaven and earth, but they were destined soon to scale to much greater heights. The angelic messengers were only the precursors, the forerunners, who were preparing the glorious way for the Queen of heaven—as the softly radiant dawn is but the herald of the brilliant sun.

PART TWO

The Lady

Age of Turmoil

In the Gospel of St. John, John the Baptizer gives testimony to the Savior entering upon His work of redemption as "the true light, which enlightens every man who comes into the world." So, too, the divine messengers of Aljustrel were heavenly precursors or beacons lighting the way of the Lady of Fatima into a sinful, chastised world to further the redeeming work of her beloved Son. She was to be another "light that shines in the darkness," for a straying humanity, even though at times "the darkness did not comprehend it."

The first of the two great crises of this era— World War I—had exploded in Europe, a continent that has suffered untold agonies in its pride of war, in the miseries of invasion, in the horrors of fratricide, in the devastation of crafty, cruel, bloody revolutions. Unhappy people who for generation after generation knew no peace nor security!

It was the year 1917, about the end of the third year of World War I. The conflict had already enmeshed fourteen nations and was about to involve even the United States of America. It was a dark and crucial hour, and the outcome was shrouded in uncertainty. People wondered when peace would come again and at what cruel price victory would be won.

The month was May, the month dedicated to Mary, the most beautiful flower of humanity. In this month in Russia, Lenin and Trotsky, arriving in St. Petersburg, were assuming command of the new social revolution that they were to spread throughout Russia as a token of the proposed, absolute triumph of communistic Bolshevism. The new movement was spreading its dread tentacles over all of Europe, intent on encompassing the world. Its propagandists adopted the universal strategy of all tyrants down through history, the strategy of attacking religion first in crushing down their opponents.

In 1917, Portugal was in a state of violent agitation. For a year it had been at war on the side of the allies. In addition, it was torn and divided internally by political revolution and religious strife.

By a series of intrigues, Freemasonry had seized control of the state, deposed the king, and was bent on driving the Catholic religion out of the land. It would expel even the King of kings from His throne in the country that had loved Him so much.

Imbued with a fortitude commensurate with the confidence inspired by the promise of her divine Helmsman, "I shall be with you all days, even to the consummation of the world," the Bark of Peter fearlessly rides the waves of persecution, hate, and disruption that threatened at times to engulf her. At the height of its fury, when all seems lost, Christ bids the stormy elements, "Be calm!" And the Evil One slinks away in terror to bide his time and remarshal his forces.

God uses the most humble instruments in His divine interference against iniquity. In the crisis facing Portugal in 1917, who would have thought that heaven had chosen for its battleground the most isolated and insignificant spot in all the land, the village of Fatima?

"What good can come from Galilee?" the incredulous asked in Jesus' times.

"What good can come from Fatima?" they asked again in 1917.

In an apostolic letter to the Secretary of State and to all Catholic bishops, dated of May 5, 1917, Pope Benedict XV wrote the following illuminating words:

"Since all the graces which God deigns to bestow in pity upon men are dispensed through the most holy Virgin, we urge that more than ever in this terrible hour, the trusting petitions of her most afflicted children be directed to the august Mother of God.

"Hence we direct Your Eminence to make known to all the bishops of the world that it is our fervent desire that mankind turn to the Sacred Heart of Jesus—the throne of grace—and that recourse to this throne be made through Mary. Accordingly we ordain that beginning with the first day of June this year, there be placed in the litany of the Blessed Virgin the invocation: *Queen of Peace* pray for us.... We have so authorized the Ordinaries to add it temporarily by the decree of the Sacred Congregation of Extraordinary Ecclesiastical Affairs by date of November 16, 1915.

"From every corner of the earth—from the majestic churches and the humble chapels; from the mansions of the rich as well as from the huts of the poor; from wherever dwells a faithful soul; from the bloodstained battlefields and war swept seas, may this pious and ardent invocation arise to Mary, the Mother of Mercy who is all-powerful in grace! To Mary may be brought each anguished cry of mothers and wives, each tear of innocent children, each longing of generous hearts! May her loving and most merciful solicitude be moved to obtain for this convulsed world the peace so greatly desired! And may the ages yet to come remember the efficacy of Mary's intercession and the greatness of her blessings to her suppliants!"

As a sign of her great pleasure in receiving the new title of "Queen of Peace," and for the complete confidence reposed in her by the Vicar of her Son on earth, who had hailed her as the "Mother of Mercy who is all-powerful in grace," our Lady would come to his assistance. Only eight days later she came in the first of the apparitions at Fatima.

She wished to demonstrate to us how closely allied to the forces of heaven and how authoritative was the voice of the Vicar, who had turned to her in trust and confidence as the "Dispenser of every grace" when he was denied and rejected by the mighty of this earth.

She came—yes, she hastened, as it were, to Fatima, answering his cry of distress and bearing a message from her divine Son, who in His infinite justice and wrath could have instantly manifested His will and visited a most terrible retribution on those who knew so well and cared so little for the effects of its provocation. But instead, He permitted His Mother to come in all sweetness and love and mercy, crowning her condescension with miracles beyond compare.

Truly, it is the finger of God—the Truth, the Way and the Life—that writes the message of Fatima. It is clear and unmistakable. The voice of Fatima is the *"Vox Clamantis*—the Voice of One Crying"* not only of the anguished advocate of earthly peace, Benedict XV, but of every righteous souls who longs for the peace of good will as announced by the angels of Bethlehem.

May 13, 1917

On May 13, 1917, from the dome and walls of the Sistine Chapel, in Rome, immortal figures of Italian art—prophets and various illustrious personages—looked down in silent testimony, as it were, on the historic event that was being enacted there. Msgr. Eugenio Pacelli, later to be Pope Pius XII, was being raised to the rank of the episcopate, receiving the full powers of the priesthood at the hands of the then reigning Pontiff, Benedict XV. About noon, when the great liturgical ceremonies came to an end, the young bishop gave his first Pontifical blessing and the distinguished audience departed.

On that same day, and at that same propitious hour on the continent, in the little mountain village of Fatima, Portugal, there began a series of heavenly occurrences that were destined to proclaim for all eternity the loving and enduring mercy of the Virgin Mary.

May 13, 1917, was the Sunday preceding the feast of the Ascension. The weather was clear and mild. The three young shepherds, Lucia, Francisco and Jacinta, attended Mass along with their respective families. Then they went out shortly after with the flock to pasture, choosing this time the basin-like hollow called the *Cova da Iria*, situated about two miles distance from the village. Arriving there in a happy, jovial mood, as usual they began to play and to sing their favorite hymns to the Blessed Virgin, revelling meantime in the beauty and the mildness of the season and in the warmth and cheerfulness of that sunny day. At midday, just when the bell of the village church would be calling the inhabitants to the recitation of the Angelus, the devout little shepherds also fell on their knees, saluting our heavenly Mother in the words of the archangel Gabriel as commemorated in the prayers of the Angelus and in the Aves of the beloved rosary.

Herding sheep is a long and tedious occupation. To pass the time both in innocence and with profit, the children had been trained and instructed by their parents to spend as much time as possible in the frequent repetition of their daily religious devotions. Heaven, therefore, was the prime object of their affections and the wide expanse of nature their daily temple of prayer. Their souls were filled with the fruits of the Holy Spirit and the grace of God. Had not heaven's celestial servants, the angels, come and visited with them in the fields and caves of Aljustrel?

Having finished their rosary and partaken of their lunch on this memorable day of May 13, the children decided to amuse themselves for a while by constructing a miniature house out of the many loose stones that lay about them. They were thus busily engaged, their happy laughter ringing through the Cova, when suddenly they were startled and thoroughly frightened by a vivid flash of lightning that cut across the sky above them. Bewildered, they looked from one to the other. They could not possibly account for this strange occurrence. The skies were clear, with no sign of an impending storm. Lucia, the eldest, remembered the many sudden squalls that had arisen in this mountainous district, preceded by lightning, but this was different. This was a brilliant, blinding light, and though the heavens remained as clear as before they were seized with an uncontrollable fear. In unison almost, their memories raced back to the apparitions of the angel of peace, of the guardian angel of Portugal, and of the priestly angel of the miraculous Communion.

But no, it was none of these now manifesting himself. These angels had come to bring celestial tidings and instructions and their mission was thereby completed. They had come to prepare the shepherds' souls for higher destinies, and that preparation had now been concluded. They had come to introduce these innocent souls to the Lord of Hosts. When the last of the heavenly Visitors had left them to return to the court of the All-High he could, indeed, have testified: "They are ready!"— ready to fulfill their true destiny, to become mighty in their lowliness and humility, to become Mary's chosen messengers in her merciful decision to bring help to a stricken world.

Little did the shepherds dream, however, on this fateful noon, as they played at house-building, that their day of destiny had arrived. Being mere children, they were stunned by the fearful flash of light they had just seen. Upon Lucia's suggestion that they should hurry home and seek shelter from what eventually might be a terrific storm, they hastily rounded up the sheep and began to leave the Cova. But hardly had they reached the outer edge of the depression when there came a second and, if possible, more stunning flash from the clear sky above them. They stood for a few moments as if rooted in the ground. Then, just a few yards away, at the very top of a small holm-oak tree, their attention was attracted by another, unearthly light, which enveloped or sprang from the figure of a lovely young lady, beautiful beyond anything they had ever seen or imagined. The general appearance of the vision was one of ineffable grace and tenderness. The very kindness of the Lady's eyes had calmed the bewildered children before she even opened her lips to address them. "Have no fear," she said, as they came closer, "I shall do you no harm."

They could not take their eyes away from the ravishing sight. Though stricken with awe, their souls feasted on its loveliness. The vision was more beautiful, more majestic than any angel ever could be. For this reason the first awakening of their blessed faculties must have told them unerringly, "It is our Lady!" Instinctively their pure and innocent hearts had recognized her whom they had always loved and honored so ardently.

Later on, Lucia, who was privileged to become the children's spokesman with the Virgin, ventured to describe the beauty of the vision as revealed in this wonderful manifestation of her love.

The Lady seemed to be about fifteen to eighteen years of age—the same as Mary would have been at the Annunciation and the Incarnation of her divine Son. She stood erect on the topmost foliage of the sapling. Beautiful and immaculate as she was, everything about her breathed of purity.

Light streamed from her figure in all directions, a light more dazzling than the sun, causing the shepherds to lower their eyes and to shield their glances. She wore a gown of purest white, drawn at the throat with a cord of gold and falling gracefully to her shapely, narrow feet, which were almost hidden in the branches of the little tree. From her head and shoulders fell a gold embroidered white mantle, similar to the cope worn by priests at the Benediction of the Blessed Sacrament. Around her slender waist was a golden cincture extending down the middle of her figure and ending in a tassel. Her hands were joined before her breast, and from her right hand there hung a long rosary with beads like lustrous pearls, adorned with a cross of silver. Her features were of an indescribable purity, sweetness, and delicacy, such as no artist could ever hope to portray. Her countenance, though comforting and reassuring to the children, was overshadowed by an unmistakable trace of sadness. And why not, with the whole world at that time plunged into an orgy of hate and destruction and the cries of innocent victims storming the gates of heaven? Does she not share all our sorrows, being the merciful Mother of sinful man, the Mother of Sorrows?

When finally the supernatural intensity of the vision had subsided to the point where the children could gaze upon and talk familiarly with the beautiful Lady, Lucia broke the rapturous silence:

"From where do you come?" she asked, momentarily fearful, perhaps, that her instinct might have betrayed her. Or was it one of those curious questions that children ask, although the answer is ever so obvious?

"I come from heaven," said the vision.

"Then why, please, did you come here?" asked Lucia further.

The Lady's voice and manner was very encouraging: "I have come to ask you children to meet me here at this same hour six times in succession on the 13th of each month until the month of October. In October I shall tell you my real name and what it is that I desire of you."

A flood of delight came over the enraptured children as they heard the promise of seeing the Lady again and again during the coming months. Jacinta and Francisco were speechless in their ecstasy of happiness, but Lucia was a frank and valiant spokesman for her little cousins. As if to hold the entrancing Lady with them as long as possible, she continued: "You say you come from heaven. Shall I come to your home some day?"

"Yes, you shall," the Lady promised, with a look of infinite love and tenderness.

"And Jacinta?"

"Jacinta, also."

"And Francisco?" came the jubilant questioning of Lucia, ever solicitous for her little companions, for heaven was unthinkable unless it included all three of these inseparable innocents.

The heart of the lovely Lady was touched. Turning from the happy gaze of the inquisitive Lucia, her eyes caressed the kneeling, rigid little figure of the shepherd-boy. In a tone mixed with boundless compassion but with a touch of motherly reproach she answered:

"Yes, certainly, and he too. But first he must pray many, many rosaries."

Finding the Lady pleased and condescending in answering all her questions, Lucia now burned with the desire to know just what had been the fate of two little friends who had died recently in the village. From the response, she seemed to gather that one was already in heaven, the other in purgatory.

But now the sweet Lady assumed the role of interrogator and made known to them her immediate desire of repeating, in substantially the same form, the question directed to them by the angel a few months before:

"In a spirit of sacrifice to our Lord, are you willing to accept everything He sends you as reparation for the sins by which His divine Majesty is offended, as a means of conversion for all sinners, and as atonement for the many blasphemies and other outrages offered to the Immaculate Heart of Mary?"

With a lively and enthusiastic heroism, Lucia replied for all three, "We are!"

And in recognition of the sacred promise just made, the Lady continued with solemn words of prophecy: "Very well, then. You are about to be laden with many sufferings. But the grace of God will assist and comfort you always."

She extended her graceful hands, still joined, as if in consecration over the heads of the little shepherds. From the points of her shapely tapered fingers shafts of mysterious light radiated toward the children, a light penetrating so intensely to the innermost recesses of their souls as to reflect them in the sight of God with greater clarity than any glass could mirror the human form. It was a visible symbol of the grace of God's confirmation at the hands of His maternal Mediatrix, the effects of which bounty was to remain with the recipients forever.

In the inspiration of the moment, they exclaimed: "O most holy Trinity, I adore You! My God, my God, I love You with all my heart!"

Before leaving them, the gracious Lady extended one last recommendation: "My dear little children, pray the rosary often, but devoutly, as you did a while ago, for the peace of the world!"

Slowly she disappeared toward the East from where she had come. As the three favored little ones later on described it: "She faded away slowly, like a feather in the breeze, without ever moving her feet."

The apparition had lasted about ten or fifteen minutes, or, as Lucia observed, about as long as it would require to say a third of the rosary.

Jacinta's "Betrayal"

When the Lady had gone, the shepherds gradually aroused themselves, looking at each other in a daze. Could it have been a dream, a hallucination? No, all three had seen her, distinctly. Had not Lucia spoken to her? Jacinta heard every word, though she could not utter one syllable of her own. Francisco had heard only the words of Lucia and none of the Lady's, but he had seen everything that occurred. No, it was more than a dream—it was reality!

Thoroughly engrossed in the discussion of their experience, they thought no more of play. For hours they could come to no end of their wonderment. Finally, toward evening they decided it was time to return home to Aljustrel. They all agreed, too, to tell no one about the Lady.

Their souls were filled with a new and profound joy, an indescribable happiness that was consuming in its intensity. They felt as though they were at the very gates of heaven. The beautiful Lady had warned them of sudden sorrows to be assumed immediately, but surely this was not sorrow—it was quite the reverse.

When they arrived at the village, Lucia admonished the two cousins before they separated:

"Now remember! Do as we have promised and do not say a word about the Lady to anybody, not even to your Mamma. Do you understand?"

"Yes, we understand," they replied.

But did they? The promise was no sooner made than it was broken.

Jacinta was seized by an unconquerable enthusiasm that gave her no peace of mind. She
thought of nothing but the beautiful Lady in the vision, and she would break out at times in a little
singsong of her own: "Oh beautiful Lady, sweet,
sweet, beautiful Lady!" And why shouldn't she tell
somebody about the source of the great joy that
filled her heart and gave her no rest? What harm
could it do? Her excited, innocent little soul could
hide its secret no longer. She went to her mother
and throwing herself into her arms, she freed
herself of the overwhelming burden:

"Mamma, today up in the Cova I saw the
Blessed Mother!"

"What are you saying, child? Do you think
you are so holy as to deserve to see the Virgin?"

But the little one insisted, "Yes, Mamma, I
saw her!"

Her mother did not seem much impressed with
the "fanciful" story.

A few moments later Jacinta came to her
mother again with an air of importance and,
disregarding her first repulse, said: "Mamma, Francisco and I are going to say the rosary. The Lady
told us to do so. And she promised to take us up to
heaven!"

The mother now began to listen more closely
to these allusions to the vision, while Francisco, no
doubt, was horrified at this early betrayal of their
pact. But Jacinta, by now, had thrown all caution
to the wind. "We must say the rosary every day—
and devoutly. The Lady said so!"

At the supper table that evening, Jacinta's
mother compelled the poor little tattler to tell the

complete story to the assembled family. Francisco, however, true to his promise, said nothing, but listened in shocked silence to the recital, only nodding his head unwillingly when asked to confirm Jacinta's statements. The next morning he fairly flew over to Lucia's house to report the betrayal.

We are told that at their next meeting, Lucia scolded the seven-year-old for her lack of self-control, but Jacinta only burst into tears and, pointing to her heart, explained, "I felt something in here. I do not know what—but it gave me no rest. I could not stand it."

Early in the day, Olympia Marto went over to Mary-Rose's house. Had Lucia perhaps spoken of seeing something unusual up in the Cova yesterday? she inquired.

"No, Lucia has not mentioned anything!"

Olympia Marto then told the whole "fantastic" story of the children's experience on the previous day, as given to her by Jacinta. Mary-Rose was indignant. She would investigate this thing immediately. And she did! That very morning she took her daughter to task, and Lucia was forced to reveal her precious secret. Lucia was rewarded with not only less credulity but with more ridicule and reproofs than had been the lot of the "arch-traitress," Jacinta.

Within twenty-four hours the little village was buzzing with the story of the apparition. It was discussed in every home and in every gathering. What presumption! What an invention! Thinking themselves worthy of seeing the Virgin Mother of God in the flesh! The little liars!

Thus it went from group to group, even in this model Christian hamlet of Fatima, until Mary-Rose, after a few days of humiliation and exasperation, took hold of her "criminal, imaginative" daughter and rushed her to the parish priest, the Rev. Emanuel Marques Ferreira.

"Right here and now, Father, you must end this terrible disgrace," the trembling woman said to him.

"But what disgrace?"

"This lying daughter of mine is the talk of the whole neighborhood!" And taking Lucia roughly by the arm, she cried: "Get down on your knees and confess to your pastor that you have seen nothing, so that he can tell the villagers next Sunday from the pulpit that it is all an untruth and put an end to this cackling!"

Falling on her knees and shaking with fear, Lucia hung her head, but insisted, "How can I say I didn't see her when I did?"

The pastor, who had remained calm and prudent as the mother's emotions mounted, felt a great pity for the little girl.

"If it be true what Lucia says, Mary-Rose, you stand high in the grace of God. And this could be a sign of His blessing upon you. Your position might be an envious one."

"If it be true! If it be true!" the distracted mother said mockingly. "But it is impossible! The girl is turning out to be a fine liar. It is the first time; but I'll show her with more than words that it is the last time too. She shall not tell any more such stories when I am through with her."

And the good mother, who prided herself on not having tolerated even one solitary lie from her offspring, took her weeping daughter by the hand and led her home.

Many years later, Mary-Rose admitted penitently that she had not spared the rod on the daughter, who was proven later to be a favored child of Mary and the instrument for so many favors from heaven upon the family. But this parental punishment was only the beginning of the Calvary of ridicule, scorn, and humiliation that was to descend upon all three children, in verification of the Beautiful Lady's warning that many sufferings were soon to overtake them.

The novitiate of prayer was ended. They were now well on their way of the cross.

The Feast of St. Anthony

St. Anthony holds a very high place in the affections of the Portuguese people. They do not call him St. Anthony of Padua, as other people do, because he is really their own, their very flesh and blood, a native of the city of Lisbon. The thirteenth of June is his feast day.

All the churches, large and small, are decorated for the occasion. High Mass is sung, panegyrics delivered, and processions formed throughout the length and breadth of the land. Even in Fatima —desolate, forsaken Fatima—he is beloved and honored in a special manner because he is the patron saint of the parish.

It was evening on the twelfth day of June, the day preceding the feast. In the home of the Dos Santos, one might have heard the following remarks between Mary-Rose and her daughter Lucia:

"Surely, Lucia, you will not go to the Cova tomorrow?"

"But certainly, Mamma, I shall go."

"You know, tomorrow is the feast of St. Anthony, and you always took great pleasure in celebrating it."

"Oh, this time it is not so important."

So, too, in the home of the Martos' on this eve of the feast of the popular saint, conversation was on the very same subject and further evidence given of youthful dissent and defection in the ranks of St. Anthony's admirers. Little Jacinta, in another transport of enthusiasm, unable to contain herself in the thought of seeing the Beautiful Lady again in a few hours, came coaxingly to her mother and most tenderly addressed her:

"Mamma, please come with us tomorrow to the Cova to see the Lady!"

But Mrs. Marto, a very practical woman, tried to make the child understand that it should be her greatest joy and duty to accompany the whole family to the celebrations in honor of the patron saint. What would people say if they were to interest themselves that day in any affair but that of the saint's?

But Jacinta insisted, "Ah, don't go to the feast! Come with us to the Cova!"

Just as the mother was about to silence her, with a gesture almost of contempt the little rebel intervened, "St. Anthony! St. Anthony! He's not pretty!"

"What's that you are saying now? St. Anthony is not pretty?"

"Because the Lady is much prettier than St. Anthony. Francisco and I are going to the Cova to see her. Afterwards, if she says we should go to the feast, we will go."

The mother now felt sorry for her. "My dear Jacinta, you will get no place with such dreams. The Virgin is certainly not going to show herself to you tomorrow nor any other time."

Jacinta was undaunted: "I am not so sure about that, Mamma! The Lady said she would come—and she will!"

However, the next morning, with never a thought on the Cova, Olympia and her husband departed at an early hour for the fiesta in the town of Pedreiras, and the two shepherds were free to obey the Lady's instructions. It was just what they were looking for.

Faithful to their promise, the three shepherds came on the morning of the thirteenth to the Cova, arriving before noon. Their hearts fluttered with joy and excitement at the prospect of seeing the lovely Vision again.

This time they were not alone. A crowd of about fifty people from the village, excited by the strange story of the apparition, and impelled more by curiosity than by faith, had gathered in the pasture. Of all the villagers (and who had not heard of the Vision?) these few risked the certain pleasures of the fiesta for the uncertainty of a visible miracle in the desolate basin. Mary-Rose, however, had no desire to accompany the stubborn children, not wishing to be any part of the fiasco that would leave her and her family once more the laughing-stocks of the village.

As the noon hour came, the children were already waiting for the Lady to appear. Dressed in their very best clothes, they knelt in the shade of a tree close to the little holm-oak, over which our Lady had hovered in her visit of the thirteenth of May. They had finished saying the rosary and Lucia adjusted her white headdress, as if about to enter a church, her eyes fixed toward the East. The two cousins suggested that they say another decade of the rosary, but Lucia warned them to be alert.

"We have already seen the signal lightning. She will be here any moment!"

Then, they all ran as fast as they could to the little green oak, the scene of the first apparition.

The Lady was there, on the same spot above the little tree, just as she had promised them, and enveloped in the same dazzling light. As if turned to stone, the little children knelt in silent, loving veneration, their eyes like bottomless wells, drinking in the eternal beauty of the heavenly Lady. Then the music of all the starry symphonies above fell on their ears, as they heard her voice once more:

"Recite your rosary every day. And after the Glory of every decade, add this prayer: 'O my Jesus, forgive us our sins; preserve us from the fire of hell, and bring into heaven all souls, especially those most in need of Your mercy.'"

In the village there was a pious lady who never doubted the children in their assertion that they had seen and talked with the Virgin, and she went to Lucia and begged her to ask the Lady, for the love of God, to cure her sick husband. Accordingly, Lucia had often prayed for the intention of this credulous woman and her ailing spouse. It was in reference to these petitions that our Lady spoke, when, at the end of the prayer above, she interposed, looking directly at Lucia:

"Let him first be converted and then he shall be restored to health within this year."

The Lady then entrusted the children with three personal secrets, one to each, with the firm injunction never to reveal them to anybody. With this, she was gone, receding and rising ever so slowly into space as she had done after the first apparition. At her feet was a small, white cloud. Deep in ecstasy, the shepherds watched the radiant figure, illuminated by a light that the Lady bore in her bosom. Lucia, pointing to the spectacle, cried out to the bystanders: "Look! If you wish to see her, she is there...there!" And all eyes turned in the direction indicated by the happy child, who, as the cloud and the Lady finally disappeared from sight, exclaimed: "Enough! Heaven now is closed!"

Even the curious audiences of villagers, the scoffers, had noticed the eastward bending of the topmost foliage of the little holm-oak, as if brushed by the hem of our Lady's dress as she departed. They heard the words of Lucia, but could not see to whom they were addressed. They noticed that during the period in which the children knelt in ecstasy they were immersed in a most mysterious light, their features transfigured, and that the light of the sun was dimmed and the color of the atmosphere changed to a golden-yellow.

Never were such things seen before in Fatima, even on the feastday of the good St. Anthony.

Many attempted to learn from the children the secrets confided to them by the Lady, but they were only assured that the secrets were exclusively for the "good of their souls," not that they would be "rich or happy in this world," but that "if the people really knew their import, they would have reason to be sad."

This resulted in much conjecturing, studious puzzling, and vain guessing on the part of the villagers as time went on. Some thought the secrets referred to the deaths and the eternal salvation of the children.

Not till ten years later, on December 17, 1927, was the real truth revealed, when Lucia herself was obliged by her spiritual father to submit them to him in written form, as authorized by Jesus in the Blessed Sacrament. The Virgin had said to her: "It is my will that you learn to read." But Lucia, remembering the Lady's promise of the preceding month, preferred that the Virgin take all three of them with her at once into heaven. To this our Lady had responded, "I shall come soon and take Francisco and Jacinta. As for you, you must remain on earth for a long time to come. Jesus wills that you shall serve Him by making me better known and loved in the world by establishing the devotion to my Immaculate Heart."

The secrets confided to the shepherds of Fatima do not end here. They await an opportune hour—heaven's own hour of revelation.

A Sign from the Lady

The fortunate spectators of the wonders of the second appearance of our Lady on June 13th spread the news far and wide. So now on Friday, the 13th of the next month, July, we find over four thousand people—certainly not all affected by superstition—assembled at the Cova, many of them having arrived there the day before.

But Lucia decided to stay away from the Cova that day because the sacrilegious doubts, as she had termed it, of some of the best people in the village had now infected her own tender conscience. The parish priest, at first neutral, now joined the ranks of those who doubted the story of the apparitions.

"I do not think this is a revelation from heaven," he had said in the presence of Lucia. "It could be a deception of the devil, too. The future will decide which is right."

The pastor's decision was a source of great confusion to Lucia. It had scandalized the soul of her who had always been so docile, so obedient and respectful toward the clergy. She was now in a quandary. Could not the pastor be right, after all? Since the knowledge of the apparitions had become common throughout the village, there had been no peace or happiness in her home. If they were from heaven, why such dissension and disorder? Such are the fruits of the devil, not of God. Was not the parish priest a wise, experienced, and educated man who knew so much more about such things than a poor shepherdess who could neither read nor write?

But oh! The Lady was beautiful, so good and beautiful!

Yesterday, she had gone to the Marto home to tell her companions of her decision to stay away from the Cova. But no qualms of conscience bothered those two young souls. They were going to meet the Lady, just as they had promised her. Jacinta, however, burst into tears.

"Why are you crying?" demanded Lucia.

"Because you are not going with us."

Firmer than ever, Lucia replied: "No, I am not going along. And if the Lady asks for me, tell her I stayed away because I fear she—is—a—demon."

The next morning, however, when the great crowd stood around the house and the hour of departure to the Cova drew near, Lucia as later revealed, "was seized by an irresistible force." As if led by an invisible hand, she left her home to seek her cousins, whom she found kneeling beside their bed, in tears.

"Why are you not on your way to the Cova? It is time you were starting!"

"We were afraid to go alone," they replied sadly. Their eyes pleaded with her. They begged her: "Do come! Please, come with us!"

Lucia pondered. Had the vision not said, "In all your trials and sufferings, the grace of God will assist you and uphold you?" Now that grace asserted itself. As if the weight of a mountain were lifted from her shoulders, Lucia literally sprang to the invitation:

"I am here, am I not? Let us hurry!"

And accompanied this time by the cousins' father, Mr. Marto, they passed out of the house and placed themselves at the head of the waiting crowd.

At the appointed hour, and in her usual manner, the Lady appeared to the happy, kneeling shepherds. The spectators, too, were on their knees, in obedience to Lucia's expressed desire that they conduct themselves in a befitting manner. They watched the children's faces closely, saw their ecstasy, made note of every change of expression—love, sorrow, anxiety, suffering—realizing despite their unseeing eyes the presence of the celestial personage, whom the children had affectionately called "the Young Lady." As in the previous visit, our Lady was telling the fortunate little shepherds to come to this same spot again on the 13th of the following month, and to recite the rosary devoutly every day in her honor. They were to pray also for the early end of the war, a favor which could be obtained solely through her intercession.

Lucia asked whether the Lady was ready to reveal her true name to them, and said the people had requested her to ask for some visible proof of the Lady's actual presence there.

The Lady answered, "Come here on the thirteenth of each month, and on the thirteenth of October I shall give them the sign they ask for. It shall be so great a miracle that the whole world will believe in these apparitions." Just before departing she added, "You will make sacrifices for sinners. And with every sacrifice include this special prayer: 'O Jesus! I do this for the love of You, for the conversion of sinners, and in reparation for all the offenses committed against the Immaculate Heart of Mary!' "

During the whole vision the onlookers noticed a gradual diminution of the light of the sun, and also a small white cloud, like that of incense, perfectly visible from a distance, coming and descending upon the children, lifting only when their interview with the Lady had ended. This extraordinary spectacle, humanly unexplainable, was seen twice later and was confirmed by thousands of witnesses whose credibility was beyond question.

When the children arose at the end of the fascinating scene, the crowd pressed upon them with a solid wall of humanity and assailed them with hundreds of questions. "Why at certain times did you grow pale an begin to tremble?" "Why did you look so sad?" "Why, Lucia, did you spring up with a suffocating cry of 'Oh!' as though someone had done you a harm?"

The two younger shepherds evaded all questions. Lucia contented herself simply by responding, "It's a secret."

"Good or bad?"

"For some, good; for others, bad."

It was, in fact, on this day that the Virgin opened the book of the future for these favored children and revealed to them the coming of the second global war* and other punishments which

---

*Twenty-two years before World War II, our Lady predicted that unless men showed some willingness to return to decency and to the observance of God's laws, they would suffer a calamity so severe that the first global war would be as

were to follow. She also gave them a twofold promise—a promise of peace to the world at strife and the salvation of souls through devotion to her Immaculate Heart. A part of this surprising revelation has already been published to the world and bears the title *The Great Secret of Fatima*. With this we shall deal more fully in a following chapter.

If the touching messages of the Virgin had infused a sense of confidence, force, and conviction into the children and into those who believed in their story, there was a noticeable growth of intensity in the trials and tribulations inflicted upon the innocents by the unbelieving. After each apparition the three, especially Lucia, were forced to undergo the same insults, reproofs, and sarcastic comments both from their families and their neighbors. How true are those words of Sacred Scripture: "A prophet is not without honor save in his own country."

While the religious authorities and the Catholic press continued to maintain a reserved and prudent silence, with just occasional expositions of their true sentiments, the liberal Masonic press occupied themselves considerably with the

---

nothing compared to it. But man did not heed her prophetic words.

On August 25, 1939, on the very eve of disaster, a peace-loving Pope, Pius XII, whose very name, Pacelli, was indicative of peace, speaking in his role as Representative of the Prince of Peace, warned that "everything would be saved by peace, but that all could be lost by war."

Yet, a week later the holocaust began. The prophecy of Our Lady of Fatima was realized. Many nations in the world plunged into chaos, and, although some of them declared their neutrality, they did not escape its devastating effects.

strange events of Fatima, giving detailed recitals of the supposed wonders, interspersed with circumstances of their own invention, explaining them with the most extravagant hypotheses and ascribing them to auto-suggestion or even to the crafty manipulations of the clergy. But the net result of their intrigue was but to spread afar the fame and the glory of the Virgin and her chosen instruments.

On Monday, the thirteenth of August, an immense crowd gathered in the rocky enclosure of the Cova. Between fifteen and eighteen thousand were there, the greater number of whom were devout believers who prayed and invoked the Lady. They recited the rosary with a voice as robust as their own simple faith and with a fervor which rendered them oblivious to the scorching rays of the sun.

As noon approached, the children, usually so prompt, had not yet arrived at the Cova. The waiting throng was becoming impatient, with increasing evidence here and there of violent agitation. Gradually from various directions came the confirming news that the shepherds were not to come that day.

"Not coming? Why? Why? What has happened?"

The Administrator of Villanova De Ourem, an anti-clerical Freemason, determined once and for all to put a stop to this "invasion of mysticism" so contrary to all existing ideas, and to this "illegal communication of heaven with earth." He presented himself first to the families of the shepherds and then to the parish priest of Fatima, showing himself affable and conversing with them most freely. After quieting all their fears and suspicions, he requested the honor of conducting the children personally to the Cova that day to keep their appointment with the Beautiful Lady. They all assented to the proposal most readily. The children especially were beside themselves with joy at the thought of riding in the Mayor's automobile, one of those big shining machines that devoured mile after mile with such amazing speed. They rode down the street for some distance to where the road forked in two directions, the one towards the Cova, the other towards Villanova. To the children's utter dismay the Administrator now took the latter road, for he had planned to arrest and confine them in the municipal prison and to keep them there until he had extracted from them the secrets that had been confided to them by the Lady in the "supposedly" heavenly visitations.

When the multitude assembled in the Cova learned of this outrage, they were infuriated. In protest, they were about to storm the parochial residence, thinking the pastor might be implicated in the plot because of his recent unreasonable attitude towards the apparitions. But they were diverted from their angry purpose and suddenly calmed by a very extraordinary interference from heaven. Up above them in a serene and cloudless sky they heard what some described later as the explosion of a bomb, others as a crackling thunder or the crash of a rocket, followed by a brilliant flash of light. The sun paled, the color of the atmosphere changed to a yellowish gold, and a small cloud, most beautiful in its ethereal form, came and hovered over the forlorn looking holm-oak now stripped to its stem by despoiling zealots. A great cry went out from the awe-stricken crowd. "Look! Look! It's a sign from the Lady!" they exclaimed, pointing to the cloud.

In truth, though the children could not be present, the Virgin thus deigned to console the gathering. Hot tears of love and gratitude flowed down their cheeks and a feeling of peace and satisfaction filled their trusting souls, that Mary had so sensibly signified to them that as far as she was concerned the appointment with the shepherds was still in force, and that she had kept it.

Perfumed Foliage

It is recorded that when Mary-Rose heard of the arrest and imprisonment of the children she exclaimed: "Serves them right! Let them stay there!" But such coldness and indifference was not so favorably received by the villagers. "Is she not Lucia's own mother? Aren't the other two her nephew and niece? Has she a heart?" True to her own character and point of view, Mary-Rose offered as her defense: "Yes, they are deceivers. They deserve this punishment. But if it is true that the Virgin appears to them, it seems to me that she will soon want to set them free." And how logical she was! By the fearless and heroic constancy displayed by the innocents in their imprisonment, after endless interrogations, as though they were criminals; after threats and tempting promises, unbearable except for the help of the Holy Spirit, their beaten captor was completely baffled by their fortitude and released them on the fifteenth of August, two days after their imprisonment.

The joy of the relatives was unbounded. Even Mary-Rose, if she were forced to admit it, had experienced many a pang of maternal solicitude that had deprived her of hours of peace and repose. She noticed the look of sadness and defeat in the eyes of the thwarted children, who had been denied the inestimable happiness of their promised visit with the Lady, and now were doomed to languish in body and spirit until she should appear again on the thirteenth of the following month. A whole month more! What a long time to wait for the enjoyment of a celestial delight that had been just within their reach and then so cruelly to be deprived of it!

On Sunday, the nineteenth of August, Lucia, Francisco, and the latter's older brother, Johnny, were herding the flock in a locality between Aljustrel and the Cabeco. It was called "Valinhos," or the place of the "little valleys," and was not far distant from their homes. Jacinta did not accompany them this time. While her cousins played together or sought their individual forms of amusement, Lucia kept a strict watch on the sheep, pondering meanwhile the harrowing events of her recent imprisonment, and wondering whether the Lady would be angry with her for not keeping the promised appointment. Thus troubled and engrossed in thought she hardly noticed how the bright sunshine had suddenly changed to an unusual pallor. Then the startled voices of her cousins brought her to her senses. Immediately she recognized the phenomenon for what it really was. She had seen it before—up in the Cova. It was the signal! The unfailing signal! The herald of the Lady's approach! Soon would follow the flash of lightning that always preceded her coming. "Run! Run, Johnny, and call Jacinta!" she cried. "It is the Lady! She will soon be here! Hurry!"

Breathless, as he arrived a few moments later accompanied by the little sister, he heard Lucia cry out again as she perceived the familiar light: "She is here! The beautiful Lady! She is here!"

The Lady appeared, standing in the top foliage of a tree somewhat taller than the one that had served her for a throne in the Cova. The Queen and Mistress of their hearts told them that she grieved for them because of their enforced absence from the prearranged meeting on the thirteenth of the month, and that, therefore the promised miracle for the October visit would be less startling than originally intended. Once more she admonished them to recite the rosary devoutly every day, and not to fail with their presence in the Cova on the next two succeeding months, at the appointed hour.

From the depths of her generous heart, Lucia, always the spokesman for the trio, in obedience to many requests, proceeded to intercede for the sick and infirm people who had been recommended to her prayers.

She was assured that many of them would be cured within the year.

But the Virgin appeared to be not too much interested in these requests, but rather, as usual, in insisting upon further prayers and sacrifices on the children's part. "Pray! Pray often, and make sacrifices for all sinners!" she said gently but slowly, that the full import of her words might sink into the innermost recesses of their souls.

Many offerings of money, and other gifts, were being deposited daily at the foot of the tree in the Cova, which had now come to be considered as a sacred shrine. Lucia asked the heavenly visitor's advice as to what purpose these presents should be applied. A part of them, she instructed, should defray the expense of two portable containers, or litters, such as the people usually carried with them in their festal processions for the collection of offerings. That the contents, at certain intervals, were to be borne to the parish chu ch, and some of the money spent in the celebrations of the Feast of the Holy Rosary, and the balance set aside for the construction of a chapel in her honor.

The containers were to be borne in solemn procession; one by Lucia and Jacinta and two other girls, the other by Francisco and three other boys, of the same age, and all were to be dressed in white.

The visitation lasted about as long as the previous ones, and, besides the privileged three, was attended only by one other person, Johnny, brother of Francisco and Jacinta, who had accompanied them to the Valley. He heard the peculiar explosion, the herald of the Lady's approach, saw his companions fall to their knees and gaze ecstatically at some figure, invisible to him, and heard the conversation of Lucia. Finally, he watched them as they arose and began to pluck several branches from the tree before which they had been kneeling.

Carefully guarding the precious foliage, they returned home toward evening.

Mary-Rose was standing in the doorway of her home, talking to a friend.

Waving the branch she carried, Jacinta cried out: "Aunt Mary! We saw the Lady again today!"

"Eh? There you go again!" interrupted the aunt, incredulous and irritated, as usual. "Is that all you do out there in the pasture, just kneel and gaze into empty space! What sort of hypocrisy is this? Didn't you learn your lesson in the Administrator's jail?"

"But, auntie, it is true! Look here! She put one foot here, and the other one there!"

And the brave little seven-year-old showed her a branch, the leaves of which were bent almost to a right angle, as if pressed by the weight of a body that had stood upon them.

"Oh, you little fraud!" said the aunt, smilingly. "Come here, and let me see for myself!"

Taking the branch in her hand, she touched it, smelled it, looked again at it, and from it to the innocent, expectant face of the child. Her expression had changed to one of mortification and profound wonder. For, from the foliage there was emanating a strange, delicious, unearthly fragrance, that soon invaded the whole room, and was perceptible to everyone within it.

It was the sweet perfume of the Immaculate!

The Footstool
of the Invisible

The knowledge of the miracles attending the apparitions became known throughout the length and breadth of the land. Especially the astounding fact that miracles were being predicted to happen at a certain hour on certain days captivated the fancy of many who otherwise cared little for the spiritual importance of the happenings. People of every class and station in life were represented by now at the site of the scheduled wonders.

On the 13th of September, the date fixed for the fifth apparition, twenty thousand persons or more had congregated. Many of them were there in open protest against the civil authorities, who, as a climax to their villainous persecutions, had imprisoned the children for several days, frightening and terrorizing them with dire threats if they would not reveal the source of these "superstitious and fictitious stories."

The air was charged, however, with a feeling of fierce devotion and defense for the cause of the victims, that threatened no good for any one who would dare to interfere with them on this occasion.

The announcement of the arrival of the children was, therefore, hailed by the immense throng with the greeting of a great victory. An aura of reverent heroism surrounded their entrance.

How, indeed, could these weak little instruments of heaven have demonstrated such firmness and valor in the face of the enemy powers except by the intervention of the supernatural? Who could doubt their sincerity, except those whose eyes were blinded to truth and reality?

The great crowd pressed in on their path from all sides, eager to see them, begging their prayers and intercessions, and seeking a place as close as possible to the remnant of the tree of wonders, which the children always knelt before during the apparitions. The eyes of the faithful were filled with tears of joy and happiness while they prayed and sang sacred hymns.

It was, in fact, a great pilgrimage for many, coming as they did by slow and painful travel from the far corners of the country.

What a sublime triumph for the three innocents and for Mary, the Virgin, the wonder-worker, the object of all their affections.

A few minutes before noon, at Lucia's signal that everybody begin to pray, the whole gathering again fell to its knees, imploring the sweet protection of the Mother of Grace.

The sun suddenly lost its splendor. The hue of the surrounding atmosphere changed to a yellowish gold. Then a great and delightful cry went up from the multitude: "She comes! Look! There! There! How beautiful!"

A small, luminous global cloud was recognized immediately as the footstool of the invisible Lady. It moved in from the East toward the West slowly and majestically. Slowly it descended to rest, hovering above the holm-oak, the tree of wonders.

The kneeling, ecstatic figures of the children were transfigured in a light that seemed to change the spot into a Holy of Holies, filled with the majesty of God.

The crowd, petrified to silent adoration at this real, visible manifestation of the Divinity, sobbed and held their very breath for fear of losing one phase of the stupendous scene.

It was evident that the shepherds now were holding intimate conversations with someone visible only to themselves. The Lady was again impressing upon the children the necessity of saying the rosary often and devoutly in order to bring about the end of the war. She reminded them that they were to come here again on the thirteenth of October, promising on that date to bring St. Joseph and the Infant Jesus with her.

Lucia implored help for the sick who had requested her intercession, and the Lady promised to cure some, but not others, because "Our Lord could not depend on them," or "because they were not properly disposed." For some, perhaps, from the standpoint of their eternal salvation, sickness was more beneficial than health.

Lucia then brought up the question again about the disposal of the accumulated money and gifts, and the Lady requested, as she had previously, that they be used as an initial payment for the construction of a chapel in her honor.

And as a tribute to the faith and enthusiasm of the assembled pilgrims, the grateful Visitor also consented that the Cova da Iria be honored from then on and recognized as sacred ground and consecrated to the memory of her presence and its attending miracles.

Finally, at the end of the conversation, which lasted about ten minutes, Lucia arose and in a loud voice cried out: "She is going away now!"

And the ball of light ascended toward the sun, was absorbed in its rays, and gradually disappeared.

During the above apparition, there occurred a most singular phenomenon, never before witnessed by the assembled people in the Cova.

From the pale but cloudless sky there came a shower of white petals, resembling snowflakes, but melting before they touched the ground, or the bodies of the astounded people.

Later on, in various pilgrimages, and on the anniversary of the first apparition of the Virgin, this phenomenon was repeated, as attested and confirmed by reliable witnesses, including the bishop of the diocese to which Fatima belongs.

Furthermore, as a proof of incontrovertible evidence, on May 13, 1924, Mr. Antonio Rebelo Martins, vice-consul in the United States, produced a photographic plate of the supernatural prodigy, verified by legal testimony under the seal of a notary public.

Wonders were heaped upon wonders with every new apparition.

The expression became quite common throughout Portugal, when people spoke of the miracles of Fatima: "Yes, I was there. I saw it with my own eyes! It is surely the work of the Virgin!"

And now we enter upon the last and the greatest of the soul-stirring spectacles, as produced in the final apparition on October 13, 1917.

The Lady of the visions had promised a miracle that would be the admiration of the whole world, but, because of the civil authorities' seizure and imprisonment of the little martyrs, she had decreed that its magnitude should be lessened. And in view of the startling circumstances surrounding the miracle that actually occurred, who dare conjecture what heaven had originally designed to manifest its almighty power?

Phenomena beyond Comparison

Predicted three months in advance, and reconfirmed in the visions of August and September, the promised miracle of the thirteenth of October was bound to attract an unprecedented number of witnesses to the mountain basin.

Men hear of momentary, unexpected, but momentous events of significance, the flash of God's finger across the sky of His omnipotence. But predicted miracles are something else again. They are a challenge to man's incredulity and to the utter perversity of his soul.

A nervous tension had seized all of Portugal. The joyful anticipation and reverent longing of the God-fearing believers was mixed with the morbid curiosity of the sensationalists.

"What will October bring?"

"And what if nothing happens!" laughed the scoffers.

Even the families of the three children were in a state of consternation. The children alone preserved their usual calmness.

Some asked them: "Aren't you afraid of the peoples' scorn and ridicule if nothing should happen?"

"No!" they replied. "We have no fear of such results. The Lady said she would come and work a miracle that all could see and understand."

The enemies of the Church were delighted with the sureness and the precision of the prophecy, thinking that now the clergy was enmeshed in an act of self-destruction, because this farce would put them in the true light of their stupidity and treacherous leadership. They gloated over the terms of the prediction: the day of the month, the hour of the day, the exact site and scope of the miracle!

What an assignment!

And everybody invited! Each to see and hear and consider for himself!

What a gullible, stupid mass of superstitious fools these Catholics must be, led by their priests!

On the day preceding this last apparition, all paths and roads to Fatima were blocked with vehicles of every description, and by crowds on foot, many even barefooted as when on pilgrimage. Some sang; some prayed; whole groups recited the rosary in unison. They passed the night on the road in the open, sleeping in their cars or on the ground, despite the cold of the October weather.

They were like a great and straggling army of souls bent on hearing the message from heaven and witnessing a miracle in confirmation of their faith. Many arrived early and waited and slept on the hard, uncomfortable limestone of the Cova. But little did they realize to what severity these discomforts were to increase on the eventful day of the final apparition.

Saturday, the thirteenth, was ushered in with a cold and steady downpour of rain that lasted all through the morning hours. The garments of the intrepid pilgrims were drenched through and through, their bodies chilled to the very bone. Fortunate were those who could find any shelter in the bogged and desolate Cova.

But, in spite of all this, crowds kept coming, new arrivals increasing from hour to hour.

Surely, the Mother of Mercy was testing to the last ounce of fortitude these trusting souls who came to witness her last appearance.

The hour of noon approached. For some, a dread hour of fearful calamity, but for the majority of them, an hour that was the goal and climax of all their hardships and sacrifices.

Finally, the word rushed from mouth to mouth, to the far corners of the basin, to them who could not see so far: "The children are here! Here come the blessed shepherds!"

And a great cry of welcoming enthusiasm went up from that mighty throng of over sixty-thousand souls.

Arrayed in their most festive garments, and accompanied by their shy and trembling mothers, the three children pushed with difficulty through the surging crowds until they came to the solitary stem that once was the little green oak tree.

There they knelt waiting for the Lady.

The rain still pelted down upon the people, who, in their excitement, ceased praying. But Lucia, the ever watchful spokesman, sensing the immediate approach of the Lady, ordered the crowds to close their umbrellas, and to begin saying the rosary.

Just then, the signal lightning flashed and the cloud appeared on the eastern horizon. It approached the tree.

"See! See! She is here," cried Lucia, and motioned all to their knees.

"For God's sake," cried her mother, anxious and excited as the crucial moment arrived, "look well, Lucia! You don't know what could happen to you!"

But the daughter heard nothing—her face became transfigured—her lips were white but showed a happy smile.

Our Lady, invisible to the multitude, as was the case in all the apparitions, appeared to the children in the usual garb of white gown and mantle, with her hands folded, and supporting the long rosary of pearls, ending in a silver cross, suspended from her hands and reaching down to her feet. But her features, today, were more radiant than ever. For this was the blessed day of revelation, the day on which the world was to learn her true identity.

"Dear Lady, who are you, and what do you want of me?" asked Lucia.

Slowly—solemnly—almost triumphantly the vision answered: "I am the Lady of the Holy Rosary! And it is my desire that a chapel be built on this spot in my honor. Continue to say the rosary every day, and with devotion. I promise, that if the people will change their lives, I will hear their prayers, and will bring the war to a speedy end."

"I have many favors to ask of you," said Lucia, mindful of the thousands of petitions that her friends had entrusted to her.

"Yes, many of them shall be helped," our Lady replied, "but many, too, shall not." These were the too-worldly ones who sought more the comforts of the body than of the soul. For their eternal destiny it was evidently better that their wishes remained ungranted.

During this conversation the people saw, at intervals, the familiar cloud of incense settle about the attentive figures of the shepherds, and slowly rise by some invisible force to a height in mid-air of about fifteen or twenty feet.

Wonder after wonder was being enacted to the gaze of the spellbound multitude.

Our Lady again took up the conversation. "I have come to ask all mankind to amend its ways and to ask for pardon for its sins." And in a tone of extreme sadness she added: "Do not add to the countless outrages by which our Lord is now offended, especially by sins of impurity."

As the Virgin was about to bid farewell to the children, thus terminating her last visit, she pointed with her hand to the heavens.

Lucia turned her head at the bidding, then cried out impulsively, "Look at the sun!"

The sky had been dark and forbidding all day, and the rain had not ceased to fall. But now, as all eyes turned upward at Lucia's cry, there was unfolded before them a series of such stupendous miracles as to cause them almost to wither away in fright and terror, as though the veil that hides the infinite and almighty power of God Himself was being drawn aside in their sight. The rain that had fallen for hours stopped, as if by some sudden command. The clouds rolled back, broke, and scattered, as if swept by a mighty wind rising up from the earth. The sun appeared, but instead of its usual blinding brilliance, it bore an aspect of silvery whiteness, so that the people could fix their gaze upon it without any discomfort to their eyes.

Then the silvery ball shook and revolved like a wheel of fire, while from its outer edges there flashed multi-colored shafts of green, red, blue, and violet. It was like a huge kaleidoscope, coloring most fantastically the surrounding rocks and hills. The crowds stood in wonder and awe, watching this stupendous miracle. The spinning ceased for several minutes, and the bewildered people were still staring at the sky in speechless wonder, when the violent jerking and spinning began all over again, with shafts of light of every color projecting from its whirling edges, in a pyrotechnical display never before seen in the heavens. Once more the people stood transfixed, watching this fearful drama in the sky, fearful of being engulfed at any moment in some great calamity.

In the meantime, the children, alone of the spectators, were privileged to witness four successive tableaus enacted near the sun. In the first they saw the Holy Family, that is, our Lady as Queen of the Most Holy Rosary, dressed in a white gown, over which was a mantle of blue. Beside her was St. Joseph, holding the Infant Jesus in his arms. Their garments were red.

Then they saw our Lord, in the fullness of His manhood, and in an attitude of benevolently blessing the people and the whole world.

In the third, they saw our Lady as the Mother of Sorrows, but without the sword piercing her heart.

In the last, the Virgin appeared as our Lady of Mt. Carmel, holding the scapular in her hand.

These manifestations ended just as the sun was about to enter the last phase of its violent swirling and dancing. For a space of a few minutes it had ceased spinning. But now again, for the third time, it gave out the same magical display, rotating with an ever increasing speed, until it seemed to tear itself away from its very foundation in the heavens, and to hurtle itself downward in a blazing, dazzling plunge of universal destruction. The people cried out in mortal terror, calling upon God and His Blessed Mother for mercy and protection: "Lord, have mercy on me!" "My God, I believe!" "Hail Mary, full of grace!" Acts of contrition were cried aloud, believers and unbelievers alike groaning and weeping and confessing, thinking that the firmament had rent asunder and that the end of the world had come.

Suddenly, the sun was stopped in the middle of its wild and unimpeded race toward the earth. The spinning ceased, and soon the sun resumed its natural place and color in the heavens.

It is recorded that when the people had sufficiently recovered their senses they found that their clothes that had been drenched in the torrential rain were now completely dried—another mark of favor from the compassionate Virgin.

The solar spectacle of Fatima is unique in the history of the Church, and for that matter, of the whole world.

Considering its magnitude, and the number of witnesses involved, it is unparalleled in any manifestations of divine power either in the Old

Testament or the New, excepting, perhaps, the many wonders attending the crucifixion of the Redeemer. It has been subjected to the most rigorous scrutiny by men of eminent learning, but, to this day, not one has come forth from the ranks of science to offer any plausible explanation for this puzzling phenomenon.

Dr. Almeida Garrete, professor emeritus of the University of Coimbra, and trustworthy witness of the strange event, offered his own description and personal opinion of the phenomenon, with the following testimony:

"I arrived at the Cova just before noon. The rain, driven by a raging wind, gave no sign of ceasing, and threatened to submerge the entire surroundings. I had chosen as a vantage point a spot on the road overlooking and distanced about three hundred feet from the place where people said the apparitions usually occurred. By now the rain was streaming down the faces of the onlookers and had drenched their garments through and through. But a few minutes after noon, the sun appeared, breaking through a dense formation of clouds that had hitherto veiled it from sight. Then I noticed that everybody was staring into the heavens, with an expression of dire calamity on their features. I, too, looked up and saw that the sun was clearly in sight, with full, rounded edges, and shining, but with no ill effect upon the eyes. Contrary to what some eyewitnesses say, the sun seemed to me to have assumed not so much the aspect of a disc of tarnished silver, as of a ball of changing, iridescent light. It was not like a moon in a clear and serene sky, which would lack the element of color in its lights and shadows. It was more like a burnished wheel, tinted like the silvery valve of a seashell. This is no poetical description. It is what I actually saw.

"It was not a sun shadowed by fog," he continued to say. "Of this there was not the slightest trace. Nor was it dim or faintly discernible, but clear and shining, from its center to its outer edges. Besides being multicolored and resplendent, the disc also presented a dizzying motion; not the lively scintillation of a star, but a rotation on its own axis that gave it a whirling, tumbling appearance. A cry of anguish now rose up from the people. With no diminution of its velocity of rotation, the sun tore itself away from the firmament, and, blood-red, seemed to plunge toward the earth, threatening to crush us all beneath its great fiery mass. It was a movement of terrific impressions! For my part, I observed these phenomena that I have just described for you, in a cool, calm state of mind, and without emotion whatsoever. Let others explain them and interpret them as they will."

Thirteen years later, upon issuing the Formal Decree of the Apparitions at Fatima, the Bishop of Leiria wrote: "The solar phenomena of the 13th of October, 1917, described by the journalists of that period, was so astonishing as to leave an indelible impression upon those who were so fortunate to witness them.

"These phenomena, that no astronomical observatory ever registered, proving, therefore, that they were unnatural, were attested by persons of every rank of society, believers and unbelievers, by journalists of the principal newspapers of Portugal, and by persons many miles distant from the scene of events, which serves to disprove any faint suspicion of collective illusion that might exist."

It should be remembered, too, that the miracles were foretold, and to the very hour and place in which they happened. And surely there is a strong argument in the fact that seventy thousand people were witnesses to them and, excepting the most rabid atheists, were forced to recognize in them the power of a divine, omnipotent Force. Therefore, we consider the prodigies of Fatima as genuine and authentic messages from heaven.

They bear the stamp of divinity, for the multitude went away believing and carried far and wide the news of the miracles, and the underlying lesson and motive of the same, that is, the message from Our Lady of Mercy, showing her powerful intercession with the Author of all mercy.

It is the voice of Fatima—which must never be stilled!

PART THREE

Unending Marvels

The Church's Approval

Persecution, an almost infallible sign of the divine source of such events, was not tardy in making its appearance in the case of Fatima. No one ever suffered more persecution than the infinitely just and gentle Redeemer. And His Church has been antagonized down through the centuries, perpetually renewing within herself the bloody passion of her Master.

It may be granted that the extraordinary happenings of Fatima allowed some doubt and incredulity to arise in the minds of many, even among the faithful, because natural prudence would certainly build up a restraining barrier of caution against any such professions of miraculous events. Popular fantasy and latent pietism are prone to invention and exaggeration, particularly in times of public calamity. But what we find most astonishing is the unjustifiable force of the explosion of hate and the systematic hostility that arose in the secular camp; a furious and passionate hate of the impious against the so-called "superstition of Fatima," even subsequent to the irrefutable phenomenon of the "whirling sun." In fact, this miracle only stimulated their fury, for the forces of evil instinctively comprehended that in the wonders of the Cova da Iria there had arisen a dangerous menace to their efforts to destroy the Catholic religion in Portugal. The public officials sought most assiduously to eradicate every vestige of substance or memory concerning the apparitions. They employed every means to keep the pilgrims away from the shrine.

They dynamited the chapel built in 1919, and attempted to destroy the little tree over which the heavenly Lady hovered in the apparitions. But needless to say, the net result of all this hostility was an increase in the faith and religious fervor of the people. They came in greater numbers than before, and organized without delay, in reparation for the indignities offered to the shrine, a huge national pilgrimage of 60,000 participants.

The Church never hurries in matters so delicate and so vastly important to her welfare, guided as she is by the Holy Spirit. Conscious of her great responsibility, she examines all things carefully and minutely so that she may give a proper final verdict in accordance with the laws given her by her Divine Founder. In fact, in the earlier stages of the movement, the Cardinal Patriarch of Lisbon, Antonio Mendes Bello (†1929) and also the new Bishop of the diocese of Leiria, His Excellency, José Correia Da Silva, issued a proclamation forbidding the clergy from encouraging or participating in any religious manifestations concerning the visions. The Church began a rigorous canonical process, in 1922, and, after lengthy and protracted studies and rigid investigations by seven persons rich in prudence and sacred science, it was solemnly declared on October 13, 1930, in the Pastoral Letter "On the Cult of Our Lady of Fatima," that the happenings at the Cova da Iria were now fully accredited, and consequently official permission granted for the external practice of devotions appropriate to the cult of Our Lady of Fatima.

The cult of Our Lady of Fatima presents its most vigorous expression in numerous and solemn pilgrimages to the Cova, to the edification of the entire Christian world, because they constitute undoubtedly one of the greatest religious movements of its kind that twenty centuries of Christian history has ever witnessed.

In 1942 twenty-five years had elapsed since the first appearance of the Virgin to the shepherds, and, as was to be expected, many celebrations were held commemorating the Jubilee of the apparitions. They began with the triumphal procession, in which the statue of our Lady was carried from the shrine to the Portuguese capital, during the memorable days from the 8th to the 12th of April. Pope Pius XII himself expressed it as "perhaps the greatest manifestation of faith in eight centuries of national history." At the passing of the Queen through the "Land of Our Lady" all work was stopped, the bells were rung, and the houses were decorated. Everyone—civil and ecclesiastical authorities, members of religious confraternities and associations, soldiers and workers, people from the cities and the countryside, the healthy and the ill— all came together carrying flowers, to form two almost uninterrupted rows of humanity 75 miles long, to offer to Mary their homage of love and unrestrained joy. Lisbon received her as a Queen coming to take possession of her realm. Six thousand girls of the Catholic Action organization, clothed in white, served as a honor guard to the Immaculate.

On the 13th of May of the same year a pilgrimage was made to commemorate the 25th anniversary of the first apparition. It exceeded all expectations, although it was a day of heroic sacrifice for the pilgrims. The weather was exceptionally cold and rainy; the means of transportation were very limited. Of the hundreds of thousands who came, eighty percent were on foot, enduring the inclemency of the weather in a spirit of humble obedience, remembering the words of the beautiful Lady, "Pray and do penance."

They had been invited by the ecclesiastical authorities to pray for the peace of a world at war, to offer reparation for the crimes of a degenerate humanity, and to present a solemn homage of gratitude for the immense benefits received by the country during the past twenty-five years, especially for the protection of the heavenly Mother, who had averted the serious spiritual and material tragedies that were tormenting almost all the other nations of the world, involving them in the destruction of a general conflict, the more painful since it was being prolonged without any promise of terminating in a true and Christian peace.

A prominent feature of this pilgrimage was the presence of 80,000 youths of the Catholic Action organization, with college and university students in the lead. Filled with the courage of their faith they reverently fell on their knees as soon as they saw the shrine, and began to recite the rosary.

Finally, at the feet of the beloved Virgin, they told her that they had performed everything she had requested—prayers, Communions, rosaries, and thousands of acts of self-denial—and therefore they could now pray to her confidently that the world be saved and Portugal exempted from the punishment of war. They swore a great and everlasting fidelity to their Catholic Faith, never to forsake it at any cost, though health or even life itself be endangered. Turning to the episcopate present there, they exclaimed: "Here we are! We want to be the first in the new crusade of redemption. Ask what you will from us for the battles of the apostolate. We are ready!"

The heroic example of these young people made such an impression that in many localities the people greeted them on their knees when they passed, a salutation once accorded to the Crusaders of ancient times.

In another pilgrimage, beginning with a series of celebrations that extended from the 13th to the 31st of October, 1942, was the blessing by the Patriarch of Lisbon of the golden crown presented by the women of Portugal to the Virgin of Fatima. The worth and beauty of this gorgeous crown may be judged from the fact that it weighs about five pounds and is adorned with almost 2,700 precious stones, including 1,400 diamonds and 313 pearls, emeralds, sapphires, rubies, and amethysts.

The actual ceremony of coronation, however, took place on May 13, 1946, as a pledge for the peace promised by Our Lady of the Rosary to be gained through her intercession.

The twenty-fifth anniversary closed with great pomp in the Cathedral of Lisbon, where the Cardinal Primate, all the Portuguese bishops, and an overflowing audience of the faithful, listened to the voice of Pope Pius XII, who, on the Vatican radio, in confirmation of the orders that Lucia had received from our Lady during the third apparition, consecrated the Church and the whole world to the Immaculate Heart of Mary.

Immediately following the Papal message, the Cardinal Patriarch, as religious head of the nation, also consecrated Portugal to the Immaculate Heart, while in every house and parish of the country the act was taken up and repeated in unison, so that all of Portugal on that day could truly be called "the Land of Our Lady."

One does not go to Fatima for a vacation, for a trip of entertainment, or a mere tourist jaunt. Whoever should go there with any of these intentions in mind would be very much out of place. One goes to Fatima "to pray, to do penance, and to beg the Holy Virgin for the welfare of those who are ill in spirit or body," as the first pages of the *Manual of the Pilgrim of Fatima* tell us.

The Cova da Iria, a rough, barren, and uninhabited terrain as of yesterday, is today the greatest of sanctuaries, teeming with life and action.

In the shade of the mammoth Basilica there is almost a never-ending feast of devout souls, especially on the anniversary days of the apparitions, from May to October, when great pilgrimages take place. The hotel reserved for the sick or distressed fills rapidly, and the boarding houses in the neighborhood are soon overcrowded.

The pilgrims begin to arrive early the day before the thirteenth of the month by every means of transportation available, singing sacred hymns or reciting the rosary. Upon arrival at the Cova, the first thing they do is to go to greet the Virgin. Therefore, they turn to the chapel of the apparitions, where, next to the altar, the Virgin is waiting for her children.

She smiles at them all, and she listens to all. They, in turn, have a word to say to her, a special petition for themselves and their dear ones, or a prayer of thanks for some graces they have received through her benign intercession.

In the obscurity of the night, the torchlight procession takes place, reminiscent of the "Procession aux flambeaux" of Lourdes. It starts at ten o'clock from the Chapel of the Apparitions. In a few minutes the dark valley becomes a sea of flames. The mass of people moves slowly and continuously, singing and answering the rosary, which a priest directs from a microphone. It is a perfect and orderly "Hosanna," a mighty and sublime "Ave," rising heavenward to the Mother of God.

A famous professor who witnessed this spectacle for the first time exclaimed with tears in his eyes: "If the Virgin had appeared here in person, she could not have been received better."

And another educated man and historian of Fatima speaks thus of the torchlight procession: "It is an extraordinary and unique spectacle, which does not have its equal in the world. This resplendent night in the Cova da Iria surpasses all that the imagination can conceive. It is truly a sacred night of light in the midst of a world buried in the darkness of sin!"

At midnight the procession ends with the singing of the *Credo*. "The spirit of the Catacombs comes to life! This melodious song, these glowing torches, this mass of men and women, in an ardent evidence of the spirit of sacrifice and prayer, is a thunderous protest against the religious indifference of our age, and a victory of eternal and holy Faith over the errors and sins of a world submerged in corruption and unbelief."

At midnight the Blessed Sacrament is exposed on an open-air altar in front of the Basilica for all-night adoration, requested by the Virgin in reparation for the innumerable sins of obscenity committed throughout the world. During the adoration the rosary is recited. The crowds, too large to find sufficient room to kneel, remain standing for hours at a time, praying for their country, for the Supreme Pontiff, for the bishops and priests, for sinners, for all the intentions of the attending pilgrims and their dear ones at home, and finally for the whole world.

For many souls, night is an evil time. A simultaneous expiation is necessary to serve as atonement for the iniquity of those hours consecrated to the devil. It is necessary to oppose sinful festivals with holy vigils. Thus from Fatima, even at night does a force of prayer come to purify nations.

An hour before dawn, that is, about two or three o'clock in the morning, the priests begin to say Mass.

On one occasion, a pilgrim priest was asked by a group of people to give them Holy Communion. They had been waiting in the hot sun for hours. He tells us:

"With the joy and unexpected privilege of a young deacon I went to the altar. Where comes this joy from within me? Oh, but Fatima is a place of grace! Here everything is different from the everyday world!—I advanced with the sacred vessel. The people lined up on either side, leaving me free passage. All of them—men, women, children—fall on their knees in the dust, in the mud, wherever they happened to be at the approach of the Eucharistic Lord. Their only anxiety seemed to be that there might not be sufficient hosts to supply them all. From every side come voices calling 'Father!' 'Father!' I admire this faith! I admire this hunger for Jesus! I admire this mutual charity! What solicitude, that no one should wait longer without Communion!"

The evangelical scene of the distribution of the multiplied bread by His apostles to the hungry crowds is here renewed and reproduced in a most perfect similitude.

At noon, the very hour of the original apparitions, the statue of Our Lady of Fatima is carried in solemn procession from the Chapel of the Apparitions to the outdoor Altar, where the Mass for the Sick is celebrated. The ill and the crippled lie on their cots or sit on the benches under the pavilion reserved for them.

After Mass, they receive the blessing from the Monstrance, while from the tribune a priest recites "Invocations" over a microphone, the crowd repeating them with indescribable fervor and touching faith.

"Queen of the most holy rosary, pray for us!"

"O Mary, Comforter of the afflicted, pray for us!"

"Most holy Mary, our mother, have pity on us!"

"Our Lady of the Rosary of Fatima, give us health!"

"Our Lady of the Rosary of Fatima, convert sinners!"

"Health of the sick, pray for us!"

"Help of the suffering, pray for us!"

"O Mary, conceived without sin, pray for us who have recourse to you!"

"Our Lady of the Rosary of Fatima, save us!"

In the afternoon the miraculous statue is carried back to its throne in the Chapel of the Apparitions. In both processions the Virgin passes through scenes of indescribable enthusiasm. The people throw rose petals in her way or wave white handkerchiefs in their acclaim. "It is another spectacle of granduer which only the Cova can present," Doctor Fischer observes again. "The Cova da Iria! If it did not already exist, we would have to create it!

"Ancient pagans used the amphitheater for evil to celebrate its triumphs. The new paganism, imitating the old, has reinstated the stadium and the amphitheater. The devil is always the same and he prefers to direct his attacks in his own way. The stadium where Mary today celebrates her triumphs is the great amphitheater built by nature in the Cova da Iria."

In the Decree of the formal approval of the Apparitions we read: "See how great is the power of prayer, and how strong is the influence of Mary, that so many souls should be attracted to an unknown, barren and forbidding little mountain village, and in a few years transform such a lifeless site into a magnificent center of piety!"

Challenge to
Medical Science

Fatima is an ever-growing miracle, continuous and imposing. Our Lady said: "I will answer your prayers!—I will heal your sick!" She keeps her promises. On the same day of the solar phenomenon she rewarded the firm faith of a mother, Mary de Carmo, 47, on the verge of death, by restoring her to perfect health. This was but the beginning; the first wave in a flood of wonders and graces that now deluge the earth.

The Bulletin of the shrine, *Voz da Fatima*, a monthly publication, published accounts of innumerable miracles. The illnesses included cancer, tuberculosis, consumption, blindness, meningitis, Pott's disease, etc. Some cures were effected instantaneously, others progressively through application of medals or images of Our Lady of Fatima, still others during the recitation of the rosary or at Benediction of the Blessed Sacrament; some during the various processions, and often in and without the Cova by the devout use of the water of the Miraculous Fountain.

Yes, like Lourdes, Fatima has a miraculous fountain, but it did not originate with the apparitions. It gushed forth four years later, when for the first time the open-air Mass was celebrated on the spot of the visions. In the huge, arid basin of the Cova, which had never held any water except the rain that descended upon it, the faithful saw a spring issue from the rocky ground. Its waters flow uninterruptedly, and are carried as thaumaturgic medicine to all parts of the world. A great circular fountain has been built on the spot, with fifteen outlets, in honor of the fifteen mysteries of the rosary, and surmounted by an imposing statue of the Sacred Heart.

In honor of Mary, "Health of the Sick," who at Fatima so prodigally shows her works of mercy, let us consider a brief account of some remarkable cures published in the periodical *Voz da Fatima.*

Forty-two year old Emilia Martins Baptista and her sisters had set out on a journey to Fatima. On the way Emilia became very ill, so ill, in fact, that the last rites were administered. Because of her poor condition the sisters decided to discontinue the journey and return home with her. But Emilia felt confident of receiving help at the Shrine and begged them not to return. In compliance with her wishes they rushed her to Fatima, and on the next day she was carried from the hospital to the Pavilion for the Sick. Here her condition became worse, and finally she suffered a complete collapse. Every effort was made to restore her to consciousness, but all in vain. After a brief examination the doctor declared her dead. But as soon as the supposedly dead woman received the Benediction of the Blessed Sacrament from the hands of the bishop, she opened her eyes, as if awakening from a long sleep, slowly came back to life and exclaimed: "But—I am well again! I am well! May Our Lady of Fatima be praised!"

Another astonishing cure to be ascribed to the Benediction of the Blessed Sacrament is that of Margarida Maria Teixeira Lopes, in the pilgrimage of October 13, 1928. For ten years she had been suffering from a disease that had covered her body with hundreds of tumors. From head to foot "she seemed to be covered with cork," as her doctor described it. In addition to this malady, she was afflicted with an ulcerous stomach, which did not respond to any cures.

At Fatima, through the intercession of the all-powerful Virgin, the "Comfortress of the Afflicted," she recovered so completely, that not a trace of her former sickness remained.

On that very same day, a woman and her little daughter, who was both blind and mute, were standing by the miraculous fountain. Suddenly, the girl grasped the medal of Our Lady of Fatima which was attached to a chain around her neck, and gazing at it intently as it were, for the first time, and filled with joy, she cried out: "Mother!" The happy child now could see and speak to her own mother and to her heavenly Mother.

Emilia de Jesus Marques was paralyzed for seventeen years and for six months had been confined to her bed, her condition becoming worse from day to day. She had a strong desire to go to Fatima, cost what it may. The doctor refused his permission. "It would be suicide," he said. But her faith and perseverance were not to be denied, and on May 11, 1929, she was taken to the beloved Shrine. She arrived on the 13th. She stayed at the Pavilion for several hours, waiting for the Mass for the Sick to begin, and for the Benediction of the Blessed Sacrament. At noon, when the statue of our Lady was borne into the Pavilion, she felt an indescribable sensation creeping over her body. Her pains disappeared, and a new flood of life ran through her paralyzed limbs. The Virgin with her sweet smile, and for whom she had waited so long, had finally come with the beautiful gift of her cure.

Never Too Late!

Faith, serenity, and steadfast confidence in the love and mercy of the Virgin of Fatima were all that was needed to convince the family of Carmina da Conceicao to have her carried to the famous Shrine, and to have her prayers answered in the form of complete recovery. "Never mind the expenses," she had argued with her parents. "I want to go to Fatima!" Dying of tuberculosis, of the kind known in medical circles as "galloping consumption," she had but a short time to live, as any brief diagnosis would reveal. Nothing in this world was left to her but hope and prayer. On June 13, 1931, in the Pavilion, that had already witnessed so much suffering, and so many tokens of Mary's sympathy, she heard Mass, participated in Benediction, and witnessed the procession. During none of the ceremonies did she feel any change in her condition. Her lungs and kidneys caused her excruciating agonies. In spite of her heroic trust and confidence in our Lady, Carmina grew sad. In the afternoon the Virgin's statue passed her again, as it was being carried back to the Chapel. Nothing unusual happened. Carmina renewed her pleadings to our Lady as her suffering increased. Just then a priest came over to the sick girls' group, noting the extremity of their plight, and was about to console them. Instead he came just in time to observe another stupendous manifestation of Mary's love and solicitude. Carmina suddenly felt better, her strength was returned to her, she experienced an overpowering urge to sit up—to leave her bed.

Just as they were putting the Statue back in its place in the Chapel's niche, the people, in their enthusiasm, in and about the Pavilion, were crying, "Miracle! Miracle!" Carmina went back home cured, as she said she would be, and glorifying the Virgin, who never lets confidence go unrewarded.

Let us consider the case of Cecilia Augusta Gouveia. It is similar to that of the preceding, Carmina's, in that the Virgin seemed to "tease" the devotees of her affection, granting them their desires after a preliminary appearance of neglect. Like Carmina, Cecilia was a victim of pulmonary tuberculosis, but complications of peritonitis had also set in.

The journey to Fatima was one long "way of the cross" for Cecilia, who was so ill that she already had received the last Sacraments. Her relatives feared she would not survive the journey. When she arrived at the Cova there was no change in her condition. Nothing had any effect on her, neither the Mass nor the procession. In fact, at the very moment of the Benediction she was in utter collapse. The afternoon ceremonies proved equally unpromising. The functions had ended and there seemed nothing else left to do but return home, with the sad prospect for her and her relatives of the same painful Calvary that had nearly ended her misery before reaching the Shrine.

After some hours of traveling, they stopped to rest and eat. The sick woman revived. Scarcely believing the evidence of her own senses, for she was seized with a most formidable appetite for food, she cried: "I am hungry!" She was given food to eat of the provisions which they had brought with them. Then she began to talk and laugh, and even to sing!—She was cured!

Thus Mary again had opened her arms of mercy and love, proving the efficacy of calling upon her in the trials and sorrows of this valley of tears. Purity and confidence are the keys to Mary's Immaculate Heart.

During the pilgrimage of May 13, 1930, a young man of nineteen went to one of the many confessionals of the Cova, and with a troubled and embarrassed air he said: "Father, I wish you would hear my confession, give me Communion and then baptize me." The priest was surprised at this unusual request, because of the order in which it was made, revealing the ignorance of the penitent with Catholic procedure in giving the sacraments.

"I came here solely out of curiosity," he confessed, "and seeking relaxation only from the press of business affairs, but seeing the faith and fervor of these pilgrims, I felt something within me that urges me to become a Catholic as they are."

On another day, the Bishop of Leiria was imparting the Eucharistic Benediction to the sick who were lying in rows in the Pavilion when a distinguished-looking gentleman stepped through the crowd of unfortunates, and came to kneel at the feet of the prelate, showing that he too desired that same Benediction. He was informed by a physician accompanying the Blessed Sacrament that the Benediction was reserved exclusively for the sick.

In tears, the man replied: "I know that, but I too am sick, in my soul." Profoundly moved, his Excellency lifted the Monstrance and made the sign of redemption above the sinner. A sick soul had found its way back to God! Arising, the penitent said: "How long ago I should have come here!" But it wasn't too late!

Naturally, moral miracles are more numerous than physical ones at Fatima and elsewhere.

Many more people are suffering from moral illness than are afflicted by physical disorders. And the Virgin, in the revelations of the mountains of Aire, has shown the greatest interest in souls: in the punishments that threaten them; in the dangers that hover over them; in the eternal happiness that awaits them—if they but prove themselves worthy of the gift. The pampered body one day must die and inherit the corruption of the grave. The soul, however, is immortal, and bound to live forever. Union with the eternal God should be the goal of all our desires.

At Fatima, therefore, Mary desires to triumph as the "Health of the Sick," the "Refuge of Sinners," the "Mother of Divine Grace," and finally, the "Queen of Peace," earthly and heavenly peace—peace eternal in the bosom of our Maker. No pilgrimage wends its way to Fatima, but that some such miracles of conversion are accomplished—miracles which are possibly more important and more wonderful than the physical ones, although they are less visible to the eyes that see only things concerned with worldly affairs.

We read in the Collective Letter of the Portuguese Episcopate: "Many sinners have been converted at Fatima. Many, who had lost all hope, have become reconciled with life. Many unbelievers have opened their eyes to faith. Many, who had completely forgotten the Church, have found her again. Lips, which indifference and neglect had silenced, are moving again in humble and silent prayer. Many are blessing the Lord, who yesterday cursed Him in horrible sacrilege." How true the statement in the Decree of the Approval of the Apparitions: "If the confessionals of Fatima were not sealed with the secrecy of the Sacrament, how many miracles of grace could be revealed!"

PART FOUR

The "Unknown Light"

The Great Secret of Fatima

Many saints have their own personal secret—and they guard that secret most jealously, often to the point of martyrdom for it. With the prophet Isaiah they exclaim: "The secret is mine, my very own!" Like the three apostles who were present at the Transfiguration on Mt. Tabor, they seal their lips with a holy silence, because they have been commanded "to tell no man what they have seen." And why? Simply because it is not to be revealed. God wills it so. Perhaps no human lips could possibly describe the secret, nor could any human mind grasp its meaning, being relevant only to future times and conditions. Would it not be a serious offense against the dignity of the confidant to divulge such heavenly messages, unless specifically commanded or permitted to do so?

The three children of Fatima were also entrusted with certain important secrets, both personal and universal in nature and they, too, were told "to disclose them to no one."

As we will see, persecution and imprisonment and even threatened death were unable to wring these secrets from their valiant little hearts. Jacinta and Francisco carried theirs with them into the grave. Lucia, in obedience to her spiritual adviser and confessor, and to the instructions received by her in a vision before the Blessed Sacrament, revealed the personal secrets in 1927 in a written statement to the Bishop of Leiria, and shortly before the outbreak of the Second World War she revealed what is known as the "Great Secret of Fatima."

In 1942, in the Silver Jubilee of the Apparitions, the ecclesiastical authorities finally deemed it opportune for the good of society in general to make at least a partial disclosure of them.

In what we know of them, however, we cannot fail to recognize the substantial nucleus, the center and focal point of the sublime lessons and directives that constitute the heavenly objective of the Virgin's visits to Fatima. That is the required conversion and the salvation of the whole world through prayers, penance, sacrifices and a continued devotion to the merciful Mother of God under the title of the "Immaculate Heart of Mary."

In the third apparition—July 13, 1917—our Lady extended her hands, and powerful rays of light shot out from them, striking the children and piercing the ground at her feet. At that moment the shepherds were privileged to look into the depths of the infernal regions.

The pits of hell, according to Lucia's description, "are like an immense sea of fire, reaching to the very core of the earth. Both demons and souls in human form are immersed in this flaming gulf. The former are distinguishable by their horrible and repugnant likeness to animals—terrifying figures, transparent, but as black as coal. Animated, diaphanous torches, they all float up and down in choking vapor and fumes, like sparks from a great conflagration and with cries and lamentations of endless hate and despair. It was, probably, at the sight of the abominable place that I cried, 'Oh!' within the hearing of the bystanders in the apparition. The vision lasted only a moment, but without the assistance of our Lady, and her previous promise to take us up to heaven with her, we could not have survived the dreadful experience."

The punishment of hell is the greatest misfortune that can befall a soul, because it is irreparable and eternal. But during the past few years, man has subjected himself to a series of calamities here on earth very much akin to the tortures of the damned. For sin—personal sins, sins of the family, and sins of the nations—has risen as a stench into the heavens, up to the throne of the Almighty, drawing His divine anger and just retribution in the form of devastating wars and destructions.

Having witnessed the unspeakable torments of hell, the children's eyes flew up to Mary, seeking help and courage to withstand the terrifying sight. Tenderly and safely she answered the plea: "You have just seen the eternal fires of hell, where the souls of poor sinners go. To save many from a similar fate, the Lord has willed to establish on earth the devotion to my Immaculate Heart. If you carry out my wish, many souls will be saved, and peace will soon return to earth. If my wish is ignored, divine Justice will exact a new and more terrible punishment. The present war[1] is about to end, but if man persists in his evil ways, in a short space of time, and precisely in the reign of the next com-

---

1. Refers to World War I.

ing Pontiff, there shall commence another and more cruel war.[2] When you shall see the night illumined by an unknown light, you will know it is the given signal that God is about to send down His punishment upon a sinful world by means of war and famine, and by persecution of the Church and her venerable Head.

"To forestall this calamity, I ask for the Consecration of the world to my Immaculate Heart, and Communion of Reparation on the first Saturday of every month. If this be done, I promise that Russia shall be converted, and peace attained.

"If the people do not heed my petition, however, impious doctrines that lead to wars and persecutions of the Church will flood the earth and the Church along with the Holy Father will suffer heavily. The good shall suffer martyrdom and many nations shall be destroyed.

"But in the end my Immaculate Heart shall triumph. The Pope shall consecrate Russia to me, and she shall be converted, and an era of peace shall be granted to the world."

For a message so explicit no comment is necessary. A sin-drenched world was warned by its Maker to mend its ways or take the consequences. God's infinite love was spurned, God's infinite patience tempted. We of the present generation have seen and felt the dire results of the Virgin's prophecy, and many of us have actually participated in the great drama of retribution that has occupied the world's stage for so many bloody and

---

2. Refers to World War II, which began under the pontificate of Pope Pius XI, the immediate successor to Benedict XV.

destructive years. Gentle, merciful prophecy has hardened into the cold, bitter facts of history.

True peace, a just and lasting and universal peace, the promised "Pax Mariana" of Fatima is not yet in our possession. Perhaps we have not deserved it. Let us pray God that we may be at least in the dawn of a new era of happy relations between the peoples of the earth, although there are many unmistakable signs of real suffering and protest among the smaller nations on account of the ideologies and power-greed of their more fortunate neighbors, who still seem bent on sowing the seeds of future embroilment.

No, we have not yet made ourselves worthy of a "Pax Mariana." God help us, and give us the grace to do so!

Drama in the Sky

In the night between the 24th and the 25th of January, 1938, an extraordinary appearance of the light of the Aurora Borealis flashed and swirled across the skies of Europe and North America.

Lucia, the eldest of the three children of Fatima, from out of the silence of the cloister that was now her home expressed the belief that this was "the warning signal" of approaching disaster, as prophesied and revealed to her by our Lady in her "Great Secret."

God's justice was on the march. Retribution was at hand. The hour of mercy had passed, and the sinful world was about to expiate its folly.

Sensing its approach and all its terrible implications—(the reader will recall her cry of "horrible, horrible!" in one of her visions)—Lucia did her utmost to arrest the calamity, hastening to remind the world of the Lady's prophetic communications, but she soon discovered that it was entirely too late for interference or postponement.

The fatal hour had struck!

Jacinta, too, the youngest of the children, had been privileged to foresee many scenes that were later to be enacted in the furious struggle that was to shake the entire world to its foundations.

Like a cinema unrolled before her visionary eyes, she saw "battles, bloody battles,"..."cities destroyed"..."nations annihilated."

The children were in the grotto on Mt. Cabeco, and were kneeling to recite the prayer of the angel, when suddenly Jacinta sprang to her feet, her eyes swinging in an arc as if beholding some far-flung series of actions. She called out to her cousin: "Lucia, Lucia!... Look! Look!... Don't you see down there!... The streets, the roads, the fields full of people, poor famished people looking for something to eat!"

How true that was in many lands—yesterday, and even today!

And what of the "innumerable armies of the dead" that were seen by the child in her vision, and the "many, too many, that are daily falling into their eternal damnation"?

These are no empty phrases or exaggerations. The Virgin did not deceive. For it is a sad reality that sin and crime have been on the increase everywhere one looks. The modern, pagan world has even lost the consciousness of sin. It refuses to believe in, or think of hell, for fear of disturbing its tranquillity of mind. The world is too wise for its own good. It refuses to acknowledge its source, cares not whither it is going, juggling with its destiny. It denies the Scriptural truth that "the fear of the Lord is the beginning of wisdom."

"Lucia! Lucia!" cried little Jacinta on another occasion near the spring, as Lucia and Francisco searched for wild honey, the veil of the future being lifted. "Did you see the Holy Father?"

"Who?" exclaimed Lucia. "The Holy Father?... Not I!"

"I saw him—just a moment ago. He was in a big house, and was kneeling at a little table. He hid his face in his hands and prayed...and he was weeping! Outside were crowds of people behaving like mad. They threw stones; they cursed and swore and said mean things about the poor Pope."

It was Pius XII, whom Jacinta saw, the Pope whose very name, Pacelli, is rooted in the conception of peace, but who was destined to guide the Church through the most difficult period since the days of Nero and Diocletian. It was he, who in an audience with Msgr. Fulton Sheen, in the early days of his pontificate, spoke these words: "If all the pain and suffering and agony of the universe could be concentrated in one person, it would not equal my affliction of being elected to the Papacy."

How thoroughly he sensed the true magnitude of the cataclysm that was enveloping the nations!

The little shepherdess also saw this Pope, in a vision in the grotto of Mt. Cabeco, "in a big church, praying before the Immaculate Heart of Mary, and a large assemblage of the faithful, both in and outside the edifice, praying with him." In visions she also learns "of the good to be persecuted— many people butchered, priests among them—until the blood of martyrs shall placate the wrath of God."

Lucia, who has transmitted these particulars to us, was always silent about her own experiences, and when asked by Jacinta for permission to mention that she had seen the Holy Father in her visions, dissuaded her little cousin from telling it, because Lucia feared the people might learn something of the Great Secret.

In her last illness Jacinta was often found with her hands on her head, immobile, preoccupied, in an attitude of seeing and hearing something that surprised her or caused her bitter sadness.

"Jacinta, what are you thinking about?" her mother would ask on such occasions.

Arousing herself with difficulty, the child looked up with troubled eyes to her mother, and contented herself with saying: "Oh, it's nothing, mommy. I was just thinking...."

But one day she confided to her friend Lucia—from whom she never kept a secret—in accents not of a tender child but rather from a soul soaring in limitless space: "I am thinking of our Lord so greatly offended.... And of our Lady who says she cannot hold Jesus' arm over the world any longer; that wars and dissensions are coming soon over the earth.... I am thinking of sinners.... Of the war that nothing can prevent." And here she repeated what Lucia had heard from her on other occasions. "So many people will die...and many, many of them will be damned forever...and many priests will lose their lives.... Many, many houses will be destroyed!...

"What grief! If they would stop offending our Lord, there would be no war and they could have saved their souls!"

And after a short pause she continued: "Just think, Lucia! I am going to heaven! And after you have seen the warning lights the Lady spoke about, you too will fly away—to heaven!"

When Lucia observed that one could not just "fly away" to heaven, she added: "I know. But do not fear! I shall pray very much for you, and for the Holy Father, and for all priests—and for Portugal, too, that the war shall never come here."

Is it necessary to add that Portugal was one of the few nations that emerged untouched by the global war?

Just two months before her death Jacinta repeated: "If the world does not repent, the Lord will send a punishment...the like of which has never been seen...and first of all Spain!" She spoke of the shattering events "that were to happen about the year 1940."

In her letters of the 19th and 30th of November, 1937—prior, therefore, to the fulfillment of the prophecies—the Superioress of the Orphanage of Our Lady of the Miracles of Lisbon, who attended the sick girl, writes in part: "This refers to a great castigation, of which she (Jacinta) spoke to me in secrecy. Within a few years many unusual things are going to happen to the world. The Blessed Virgin said if men would repent, our Lord would pardon them at once, but if they did not repent, the punishment was sure to follow."

The little shepherdess was not at all mistaken.

A Striking Document

Although heaven's design in the apparitions, secrets, and prophecies of Fatima was manifested in part by merciful warnings, and consequently castigations for man's perversity, it is equally apparent that the full scope and depth of the mysteries involved still defy our frail, human powers of exploration.

In contrast to the eternal punishment merited by some, we find that the temporal castigation for not heeding the Virgin's warning could be mitigated and abbreviated.

We learn that our Lady's intercession obtained an abbreviation of the first global war as an award for the daily recitation of her rosary in a humble plea for peace. She had promised in 1917 to bring all combatants home soon from the fields of battle and in 1918 the war was ended.

Her maternal influence was conspicuous also in the conflict brought to a close in 1945. Many of its major events shall henceforth be commemorated simultaneously on feast days that had been set aside by the Church for special devotion in her honor. Many, too, coincide with events connected with the story of Fatima, as if the Virgin wished to attract our special attention to the prophecies made in 1917.

Without her mediation the second global war might have been prolonged indefinitely, with a considerable increase in the already staggering losses of human lives and national wealth. Consider her own words: "By giving heed to my request, this punishment," meaning World War II "shall be mitigated...and finally my Immaculate Heart shall triumph...and a long era of peace shall follow!"

An era of peace is not synonymous with a cessation of hostilities, or a mere armistice, or a peace treaty. The destruction of one's enemy does not mean peace. The systematic enslavement of whole nations, the brutal expulsion of peoples from the soil of their fathers, the cold-blooded starvation of millions is not peace. The exchange of one form of totalitarian policy for another is nothing but a mockery of peace. It can never be a "Pax Mariana." It is more a disparagement of Mary's intercession and God's infinite mercy.

Mary's program is prayer, penance, and sacrifice. Incessant prayer and continual penance—to obtain pardon, mercy, and salvation.

Lucia confirmed this at the time it was proposed that she divulge, in part, the "Secrets of Fatima." She said: "Some people may be of the opinion that I should have revealed these facts at the very outset, because now their value has diminished. That were true if God presented me to the world as a prophetess. But that was not His intention. Otherwise, instead of binding me to a secrecy which was approved by His appointed Ministers, He would have commanded me to speak. I think the Lord wished to serve His purpose through me, solely to convey to the world the necessity of avoiding sin, and of offering prayers and penances as reparations for the countless offenses against His divine Majesty."

Through the instrumentality of her appearances, our Lady revealed that everyone, without exception, should observe these three things:

1. A return to God, with a denial of ourselves.

2. An avoidance of sin, especially sins of impurity, and the occasions of them, by fighting our evil passions and propensities.

3. The observance of God's commandments— all of them!—and the commandments of His Church.

This requires many sacrifices. But with Jesus and Mary's help, it can be done, and many are doing it every day.

They are God's heroes!

The true hero on the field of battle is not he who is ever mindful of his own welfare, but who recognizes the dangers surrounding his fellowman, and who immediately goes to his neighbor's rescue when he falls.

Our Lady of Mercy delights in fostering and developing in "men of good will" an apostolic spirit for the salvation of their unfortunate brethren.

She tells the little shepherds repeatedly: "Pray, pray for them (sinners)! And offer sacrifices for them! So many souls are being lost because no one prays for them!"

We are all, regardless of the difference of birth, children of God, redeemed by the same precious blood, destined heirs of heaven, and members of Christ's Mystical Body.

Our Lady taught the children to say this prayer in all their sacrifices: "I do this, O Jesus, for love of You! For the conversion of sinners, for the Holy

Father, and in reparation for all the offenses committed against the Immaculate Heart of Mary!"

Being true children of Mary, the shepherds were also taught by her (and we learn from them), to recite the holy rosary daily, in a spirit of apostolic zeal: for peace, for sinners, for the world, for the Church militant and suffering. She invited them to insert after every decade a brief prayer: "O Jesus, pardon our sins and preserve us from the everlasting punishment of hell. Bring to heaven all souls especially those most in need of Your mercy!"

The words that summarize the whole essence of the message of mercy, and that were engraved most deeply in the heart of Lucia, were uttered by the Virgin just prior to her last farewell, when, in accents of untold sadness, and in a voice of supplication she exclaimed: "Mend your lives, that you may obtain pardon for your sins! Do not grieve our Lord any more, who is already so much offended."

Finally, as a most powerful aid in this reconstruction of our spiritual lives, the Blessed Virgin recommended a universal consecration and devotion to her Immaculate Heart, the refuge and salvation of all mankind. To expiate the sins of a carnal world, and to shield us behind the barrier of her Virginal Purity, she revealed that it would be a most pleasing practice to set aside in her honor the first Saturday of five consecutive months in the year. (The subsequent chapters contain more particulars concerning this devotion.)

The world is sick, dazed and bankrupt, physically and spiritually, after many long years of destructive conflict and atrocities not recognized even in warfare. The best minds are occupied with thoughts and plans for a rebuilding of its material strength. But most of all, it needs a spiritual awakening and a spiritual assistance. The vanguard of this great army of spiritual warriors should be the children of Mary, faithfully following the precepts and teachings as laid down in the apparitions of Fatima, and revealed to three pure and innocent children for the good of all of us.

"Blessed are the clean of heart, for they shall see God!"

In a letter dated April 20, 1943, to the bishop of Leiria, Lucia wrote that the Blessed Virgin had condescended to make additional revelations concerning the war and the various means to be employed in placating Divine Justice, that the world might be spared a new or protracted punishment. The letter reads in part: "The Lord is pleased with what has been done so far." (Evidently, she refers to the consecration of the world and the Church to the Immaculate Heart of Mary by Pope Pius XII a few months previously.) "However, according to the desires of the Holy Father and of the Episcopacy, there remains much more to be accomplished.

"Our Lady promised that the war would soon be terminated, and that Russia would be converted, not immediately, but on condition that Spain take heed of the Lord's request and mend her ways. Failing this, Spain is to be persecuted anew, and Russia herself, prior to her conversion, is to be the punitive instrument of God's retribution.

"The feeble efforts of man to appease God's righteous anger have been accepted, but it is a bitter regret of His Infinite Love and Mercy that so few souls are in the state of grace or disposed to do whatever is necessary to keep His commandments. For the observance of them constitutes actually the penance that God has been asking for; the sacrifice that every soul must impose upon itself, for the fulfillment of its destiny; the effort necessary for the proper execution of Divine Law.

"This thought must be firmly established in our mind: it is not necessary for salvation that we subject ourselves to great penances and austerities, the very thoughts of which are discouraging and conducive to perpetual tepidity. The penance or self-mortification that God actually requires of us consists of practices and sacrifices that enable us to preserve sanctifying grace in our souls, by keeping the commandments and performing the duties proper to our state in life."

These are plain words, true and encouraging. In the world as it is today it is impossible to live in a state of sanctifying grace unless we have a plan for living. No half-way, haphazard measures will do. If we believe in the efficacy of the sacraments as the channels of divine grace, then we must use them often and perseveringly, just as the body must be daily nourished. We must derive our daily strength from Mass and the sacraments. To achieve our daily victory over sin and temptation we need to frequently approach the sacrament of Penance, where grace is restored in our souls, and go to Communion, where the Food of all foods is given, the body and blood of our Lord Jesus Christ.

"Seek first the kingdom of God—and all else shall be given to you!"

All else! Everything!

PART FIVE

The Song of Innocence

Joys and Sufferings

Among the many moral miracles so characteristic of Fatima, one alone, attributed to our Lady, is sufficient to establish the truth of the apparitions, namely, the profound change that was worked in the souls of the little shepherds from the moment they first saw and talked with the Blessed Mother, and the saintly, angelic lives they led afterwards, in the spirit of the messages transmitted to them.

If we study this transformation, and permit our minds to be enlightened by their young lives, we cannot fail to arrive at an intimate and profound comprehension of the purpose of the Virgin in her messages to the world from Fatima.

The manner and means of these transmissions—simple, direct and understandable, and at a time when all hearts had need of rising to a higher plane of spirituality—constitute an eloquent lesson, an irresistible stimulus to the conversion and spiritual progress of every willing soul.

We must recognize them, and study them, as privileged souls.

Apart from the Old Testament, was not the first manifestation of the Messiah in the New Covenant made to the poor lowly shepherds by the angel choirs of Bethlehem, bidding them to come and adore the newly-born Son of God?

Down through the centuries that followed the dawn of that first Christmas morning, is it not a remarkable fact that the Virgin, in the greater number of her apparitions, has chosen innocent, unpretentious shepherds, as the instruments of her revelations to mankind? She seems to have a marked predilection for these rugged souls, in perpetual memory of—or perhaps, as a reward for—the kindness and comfort they brought to her on that lonely night when Christ her Son was born.

So, too, at Fatima the heavenly privilege of gazing into the eyes of the all-beautiful Lady was reserved for three young shepherds. They were unlettered, and could boast of no earthly advantages whatever. Their exclusive knowledge came from the celestial Mother of God herself, and from the intimate action of the Holy Spirit on their souls.

Of the three children the one that seems to have received the most graces was the youngest—Jacinta, only seven years old, who, before the apparitions, had been most capricious and obstinate in her behavior. Up to the time of the heavenly visitations, all three were ordinary children, pleasing and robust in appearance, but with all the little faults and normal tendencies of the average child. They loved to play, and sing, and dance, especially Jacinta. They would even shorten their prescribed prayers, in order to have more time for play while watching the sheep. But their favorite mode of self expression was dancing. And why not? In Fatima, as elsewhere, the dance is a favorite pastime of young and old—in the home, in the gardens, at play, and on every festive occasion. With the children of Fatima dancing was a most innocent diversion. In the words of the Apostle, "Everything is pure to the clean of heart." Contrary to some of modern perversions, the dance was an expression of joy and innocence, not a contamination of body and soul.

Being healthy, normal children, and inseparable companions, it is only natural to assume that the three shepherds could not pass all their time in perfect contentment and unison of spirit. At times Jacinta, the little rebel, could be a source of much irritation to others. From the writings of Lucia, we have the following account of the little one's periodical outbreaks: "Prior to the events of 1917, excepting the fact that we were cousins, I had no particular reason for preferring the companionship of Francisco and Jacinta. On the contrary, they displeased me because of their childish susceptibilities. The slightest argument among the children was sufficient to back Jacinta into a corner like a stubborn mule, and no amount of coaxing could induce her to come out again unless she was permitted to have her own way."

Francisco and Jacinta, however, were much attracted to Lucia, and preferred her friendship and companionship to that of any of the other boys and girls in the neighborhood. They recognized something in their older cousin that made them look up to her as a model. As Jacinta expressed it one day to Lucia: "We do not like to play with other children because we might hear nasty words that are sinful and make the Infant Jesus weep."

In spite of their own faults, the children were filled with a love for their parents and relatives and for Jesus and His Blessed Mother. And they were faithful in their prayers. They prayed often, as only children know how to pray. If they quarreled, or were peevish and obstinate towards one another on certain occasions, they soon forgot their little differences and became friends again.

How then are we to understand these contrasting qualities of their natures? Because they were sensitive of heart and the good Lord had endowed them with wholesome characters beneath whose rugged exterior there was a spirit of amiability and graciousness.

Speaking of Jacinta, Lucia affirmed in her writings: "I am indebted in great part to her companionship for the preservation of my innocence."

She tells several little stories about her young cousin, none of which is lacking in deep significance.

"On the Feast of Corpus Christi," writes Lucia, "my sister used to dress several little girls as angels, to march in the procession beside the baldachin, and to strew flowers before the Blessed Sacrament. Fortunately I was always chosen to be one of them.

"Once, as my sister was preparing my dress for the occasion, she explained to Jacinta that the Feast of the Blessed Sacrament was soon to be celebrated, and that I was to participate in it as a flower girl. The little one begged me to seek a like honor for her from my sister. We united our pleadings, and my sister consented. A dress was made for her and then she was instructed how to strew the flowers before Jesus.

" 'Will we be able to see our Lord?' asked Jacinta with great interest.

" 'Certainly!' replied my sister. 'The pastor carries Him!'

"Jacinta was overjoyed and kept asking how long must she wait until the coming of the feast day.... Finally the great day arrived, and Jacinta's cup of happiness was filled to overflowing. We went together to the altar and took our places at the side of the baldachin, each with our golden basket full of flowers. The procession started. At certain intervals, prearranged by my sister, I threw my flowers, but I noticed that Jacinta made no move at all to strew hers, and paid no attention to my signals to do so. Instead, she kept her eyes fixed on the priest. She saw nothing else.

"At the end of the ceremonies she was asked why she had not strewn her flowers. She answered sadly: 'Because I didn't see Him!' The Lord Himself must have smiled down on her angelic innocence. Then after a few moments of puzzled thought she asked me: 'Well, did you see the Little Jesus?'

" 'No, but you don't understand, He was there, hidden in the Host! The same as we receive in Holy Communion!'

" 'Do you talk to Him at Holy Communion?'

" 'Sure, I talk to Him.'

" 'But why didn't I see Him?'

" 'Because He is hidden.'

" 'But how do so many people receive the hidden Jesus at one time? Does each one get a portion?'

" 'Oh, no! Even though there are so many hosts, Jesus is in each one of them!' "

Then, having got all the information that Lucia could give her, the little one inquired with great enthusiasm: "May I go to First Holy Communion like you did? May I, too, receive the hidden Jesus? May I, too, talk to Him?"

One of the games the shepherds loved to play was called "Pledges." The winner was permitted to impose a penalty on the loser who agreed to accept it as a penance.

Jacinta generally obliged the loser to go and catch a butterfly and bring it to her, or to collect for her a few flowers that she admired.

One day they were playing this game in Lucia's home. Lucia won, and the penalty she demanded was that Jacinta should go and kiss Lucia's brother who was writing at the table.

Jacinta objected: "That? No! Give me another penance! Why don't you send me to kiss Jesus there?" and she pointed to a crucifix hanging on the wall.

"Alright! Get a chair, take it down and bring it to me. On your knees you must give three kisses: one for me, one for Francisco, and one for yourself!"

"To our Lord I'll give as many kisses as you want!"

And she took the crucifix and commenced to kiss it and hug it to her breast with such tender devotion and love that years afterward Lucia said she had never forgotten the beautiful gesture.

Having restrained her impulse, Jacinta stood and contemplated the sacred image in thoughtful silence, and then turned to Lucia and asked sorrowfully: "Why is the Lord nailed like that to the cross?"

"Because He died for us!"

"Tell me all about it."

Lucia knew the story of Christ's passion very well, and therefore had no difficulty in telling it to the little cousin, down to the last particular. Jacinta listened intently, thoroughly fascinated, but then she finally broke into tears. "Poor Jesus," she exclaimed, "I will never in my life commit a sin, because I don't want Him to suffer for me!"

Such was the life of the three shepherds prior to the prodigious events of 1916 and 1917. But when our Lady asked them if they were ready to offer themselves to God, to make sacrifices for His sake, to accept all sufferings He would send them in reparation for the sins against His majesty and her Immaculate Heart and for the conversion of sinners, their prompt answer was: "Yes, we will!"

Out of pure love for her and the good Jesus, they accepted this mission of reparation, willingly and with full simplicity.

That was the first step!

Our Lady accepted their offer, but hastened to add: "You shall soon have much to suffer, but the grace of God will give you the necessary strength."

On that very day their trials began and remained with them for the rest of their earthly days.

From the moment that the people of Fatima first learned of the apparitions of the Lady, the innocent shepherds were branded as liars and hypocrites, even by their own mothers. In their own homes they were scolded, vexed, and derided. Convinced of their children's lying, the parents went so far as to inflict severe bodily punishment upon them whenever they insisted upon having seen the Lady in the apparitions.

The Cova da Iria contained a small piece of fertile ground owned by Lucia's parents. It was useless now for cultivation, having been badly trampled by the crowds who went there to attend the apparitions.

Sick and depressed by the attitude of both her family and the villagers, Lucia was unable to take care of the sheep, and consequently, they had to be sold, thus adding to the mounting difficulties in the family.

Her sisters bitterly reminded her of the misfortune which they believed had descended upon them because of her lies, deception, and told her: "Now you can eat what you have sown in the Cova!"

And at mealtime, even Lucia's mother, worried and harassed by the gossip and excitement, would tell her: "You there, if you want to eat, go to your beautiful Lady for your food!"

"Finally," she revealed later, "the tension became so great that I dared not take even a mouthful of bread to eat.... I hope our Lord accepted my sufferings, which I always offered up to Him, content that I could sacrifice myself for Him and for the sins of others."

But the fiery persecution sometimes became unbearable, and the little soul weakened in her determination to become a living sacrifice. Providentially, then, cousin Francisco would come to her aid, telling her that the Lady had warned them of these tribulations, and that they must endure them for Jesus and the Immaculate Heart, because they were so sad. And if we can console them with our sufferings, he would add, then we should be happy.

There were certain women in the village who scoffed at the apparitions. They argued against them continuously, and had no patience with anyone who professed to believe in them.

"Some of these women," says Lucia, "publicly proved their disgust by actually beating me when they met me on the street.

"Francisco and Jacinta were periodically subjected to the same treatment until their parents finally made it clear to everybody that they would have no more of it. Oftentimes, however, my little cousins were moved to tears at the sight of people punishing me.

"One day, the little one said to me: 'I would be happy if my parents acted like yours, so that the people might beat me. Then I could make many more sacrifices for the good Lord.' "

The Indignant Administrator

When it became known that the vision had confided certain individual secrets to the children, with the strict injunction to reveal them to no one, the administrator of Villanova de Ourem, the prefecture of Fatima, vowed to obtain the information from them by fair means or foul, and subjected them to a treatment that was little short of criminal.

One day an order went out from the Municipal Office to the parents Marto and Dos Santos, commanding them to appear before the Administrator on the following morning at a certain hour, accompanied by the offending visionaries.

The villagers all trembled at the very thought of being summoned before the Administrator, for in those days it was disastrous to fall into the hands of a man so cruel and ambitious, the head of the Masonic and republican forces, and whose word was law.

On the appointed day, Lucia and her father departed early on their journey to the office. They stopped at the Marto home to join company with the uncle and cousins, but Mr. Marto refused to take his children along with him, stating that they were too young to know what the whole procedure was about.

Profiting by a slight delay in the preparations Lucia narrates: "I ran to Jacinta's bed to say farewell. Doubting whether I should ever see her again, I embraced her. She began to cry, but reassured me with the promise that she and Francisco would go daily to the spring and pray for me. And if they kill you, tell them that I and Francisco are just as guilty as you are, and that we are ready to die also!' No one can imagine how much they suffered that morning thinking I was to be killed. But what hurt me most was the utter indifference of my parents.

"The Administrator asked me many questions and demanded that I reveal my secret. But when he finally realized that he could not pry the message from me, he let me go, saying that he would get the information at any cost, even if he had to kill me. He reproved my uncle sharply for having disobeyed his order to bring the children with him, and then he dismissed us.

"Arriving home that same night, I immediately went to the spring. There I found my little cousins on their knees, their faces covered with their hands—sobbing. They were surprised to see me.

" 'Is it you—here? Your sister just came to the spring for water and told us that at this very hour you were to die. We began to cry and pray for you!'

"Then they embraced me joyously. After much questioning, Jacinta exclaimed: 'See! We don't have to fear anymore. The Lady will always help us. She is our big Friend.'

"Several days later," Lucia continues, "three horsemen came to the house and questioned us again. Upon leaving they warned us: 'You had better make up your minds to tell your secrets to the Administrator—or you will all be killed!'

"The threat was entirely lost on Jacinta, for her face lit up with happiness as she exclaimed: 'Good! I like the good Lord and the Lady. Now we can soon be with them.' "

The news that the children's lives were endangered soon spread throughout the village, and beyond it, so that one of Lucia's aunts, who lived in another municipality, offered to take them into her home to hide them away from the authorities. But the shepherds refused to go, saying that if they were to lose their lives the sooner they would go to heaven.

On August 13, 1917 (to be remembered as the day appointed for the fourth apparition) the children were again taken into custody by the Administrator, to be interrogated and subjected to all sorts of threats in an effort to wrest their secrets from them.

When they persistently refused to give him the desired information, the magistrate had them locked in a private room, saying: "You will be free again only when you decide to talk!"

For any children of their tender age, this would have been a frightening experience if they were not forewarned, as these were, by celestial communications that much suffering was to befall them, and that heaven's strength would fortify them in all their afflictions. Nevertheless, childlike and immature, as they were, they were not entirely devoid of fright and terror, Jacinta being only seven years of age at the time.

For them, who had spent all their daylight hours out under the great dome of the heavens, the thick walls of the prison were menacing. The heavy locked doors and the interminable hours clutched at their lonely little hearts. The shades of evening made a spooky abode of their cell, and the night, a dungeon. Uncertainties of all sorts filled their bewildered minds.

Huddled forlornly in one corner of the room, they threw their little arms around each other, as if to symbolize one mind, one force, one general cause, for which they were ready to give up everything—even their lives, if it came to that.

Remembering their vow to the Lady, that they were "ready" to accept all sufferings in a spirit of sacrifice, they prayed the rosary adding the words that she taught them in the apparitions: "All for Jesus and the Immaculate Heart, and for the conversion of sinners."

They continued in this holy ordeal of the day, and with the name of their beloved Mother and protectress on their lips, they fell asleep, under the gaze of their guardian angels.

Early on the following morning they were awakened by the noise of passing footsteps in the outer corridor. Presently, a key was turned in the lock and the door swung open. Before them stood a woman—an old and ugly woman. The frightened little prisoners sprang to their feet, wondering who this strange figure could be, and what could be her intentions. But the old hag was reassuring, and tried her best to be friendly. Then thinking they were to be set free, they ran to her, only to learn that she was a temptress, sent by the magistrate to entice them into divulging their secrets. Thinking that a night of terror in a lonely prison cell would render the children a willing prey to his wily scheme, the old woman had considered her task an easy one. But she had reason soon to change her mind and attitude.

From promises she proceeded to dire threats and scoldings. The task was not so easy, after all. The children were adamant, and refused to tell her anything. Thoroughly beaten, she finally left the cell, her strident imprecations ending with the slam of the heavy door.

A few hours later, an official came and led them away to the Administrator's office.

Again they went through the grind of endless questioning. It had become an all-devouring ambition in this magistrate to find some pretext for attacking and injuring the Catholic faith, in and beyond the community, by discovering some crime or scandal that he could pin on its clergy. This was an ideal setting, and he swore that he would succeed in his insidious designs. These visionaries, these hysterical, unbalanced, unlettered shepherds were to be instruments of his plans.

All of this talk of apparitions and miracles was nothing but priest craft—a money-making scheme, and he would expose it as such. Now he had the priest's tools in his hands, and nothing was to be left undone to search for the real instigators of the swindle.

He prefaced the hearing, as usual, with the most glittering promises. He questioned them all together, then separated them, made notes of their answers, and brought them together again in an attempt to confuse them and thus lead them into contradictory statements. But all to no avail. The children had but one story, and they never deviated from the truth.

Then a bright idea struck him. Taking several pieces of gold coins from his pocket, he flashed them before their eyes, smiling, and inwardly gloating at the thought that this was one bribe they could not possibly refuse.

"Tell me everything," he coaxed, "and this gold is yours!"

They told him the whole facts of the apparitions, simply, directly, without deviation or contradiction.

"But what about the secrets, the famous secrets that everybody talks about?"

"We are not allowed to tell them to anybody."

"Why not?"

"Because the Lady forbade us to tell anybody, and the Lady is greater than all the administrators in the world!" How brave and naive they were!

Thereupon the baffled magistrate began to lose his head—and his dignity.

What were these beggarly little mountaineers trying to do? Make a fool of him, the highest official of the district?

Angrily he ordered his agents to lock them up again. And why not? This was his sole remaining weapon—force against logic.

They were sentenced to the public jail and warned that if they had to be sent for again, they would be burned alive.

The Chamber of Torture

The Administrator's wife—like Claudia Procula, the wife of Pilate—was a woman of mercy. She pitied the poor, hungry, bewildered children, without nourishment at least for twenty-four hours. As they were being led to prison, she took them into her kitchen and gave them some food. We are not sure, whether she, like Claudia Procula, interceded with her husband in the cause of justice. In any event, they were led away to the jail.

Some of their fellow prisoners, neither knowing who they were, nor for what crime they were being imprisoned, were kind to them, and sought to comfort them as much as possible. But the strangeness of the dark and gloomy cell, with its high walls and iron-barred windows, the aspect of the older prisoners, with their long beards, fierce and emaciated countenances, had such an effect on little Jacinta that she withdrew to a corner of the cell and began to sob piteously.

Lucia went to her and whispered words of encouragement. Pressing the little one's head to her breast, she said, "Why do you cry, Jacinta?"

"Because our parents will not be here to embrace us before we die! No one has come to see us!—to help us! They don't love us anymore.... If I could only see my mamma!"

The hour of prediction had come—the bitter chalice of persecution and suffering was almost full to overflowing.

145

But with a firmness and bravery far beyond his tender age, Francisco approached his sobbing sister and reminded her that she should keep her promise to the Lady to accept all sufferings as sacrifice for sinners.

"Yes, I know," said Jacinta, "but I am thinking of papa and mamma, without wanting to cry."

"But if we can't see them, we can't help it. Wouldn't it be much worse if we were never to see the Lady again? That's what I am afraid of. But that, too, I would offer up for sinners!"

Thereupon, Francisco fell on his knees, folded his hands, and with his eyes raised toward heaven, as if he were in church, he made the "offering" that had been taught them: "O my Jesus! This is all for You, for love of You, and for the conversion of sinners...."

Jacinta, overcome by his exemplary behavior, knelt and joined him in prayer. Immediately she recalled the vision she once had had of the Holy Father in a large house, kneeling in prayer, weeping as she now wept. Accordingly, she added to her offering: "And for the Holy Father, and in reparation for the offenses committed against the Immaculate Heart of Mary."

The eyes of the elder, hardened prisoners opened wide in wonder at the sight of this behavior, never before witnessed in the horrid cell. Some were moved to tears; others equally affected, began to console the shepherds. Those who had managed to learn the story of their arrest advised them to go to the magistrate and tell him all—secrets or no secrets, Lady or no Lady—the main thing was to get out of the dirty jail. That was no place for poor young children like them, they said.

Jacinta, assuming the role of spokesman for the three, rejected the well-meant but offensive counsel with a curt: "We would rather die!"

About noon, the little prisoners remembered that they had not yet recited the rosary. The sharp eye of Jacinta had discovered a nail sticking out of an empty wall of the cell. Taking from her neck a medal of our Lady that she always carried day and night, she gave it to one of the elder and taller prisoners to hang up for her.

Down on their knees went the shepherds—exactly as they used to do in the pastures, or at Lucia's spring, or in their own little bedrooms at home—and they began to pray.

Slowly, one by one, moved by the extraordinary piety of the brave little prisoners, all were on their knees around them, their rough voices mingling with the silvery accents of the innocents, in the praise of the Mother of Grace.

In the afternoon the children were taken out for another hearing, more torturous than any prior one. Finding them still unyielding in their determination to preserve their secrets, the Administrator had recourse to a final, diabolical scheme. Springing from his chair in a furious outburst of anger, he pounded the table like one obsessed, and shouted: "Since you refuse my offers, then you shall take the consequences!" Motioning to one of his assistants he cried: "Prepare at once a kettle of boiling oil. I'll fry these rebels alive—if they refuse to talk!"

They were ordered into an adjacent room. By now, the children were almost frightened to death. This time, surely, nothing could save them.

In a few minutes the door of their room was violently opened, and the Administrator himself summoned Jacinta by name.

"Come here, you! You'll be the first to fry like a fish, if you don't speak out!" The little martyr, who a short while before had cried because she could not see and embrace her papa and mamma, now proceeded, without a sign of a tear, to follow the executioner. But turning to Lucia and her brother as she left, she whispered: "I won't tell him a thing!"

She was taken to another room.

"If they kill us," said Francisco to Lucia, strengthened by his little sister's bravery, "so much the better!... A little while now, and we will be in heaven!" And then after a few moments of silence, as though fearful of being cheated of martyrdom: "I hope God helps Jacinta not to weaken! I'll say a Hail Mary for her.

"...Pray for us, sinners,...at the hour of our death...."

Lucia said nothing, as silent prayers of supplication and resignation fell from her pure, firm lips. Like a little mother, she had always been the mainstay for the youthful cousins in times of danger and advice, but now, in this difficult hour, no supervision was necessary. Her house was in order. The fortitude, yes, the eagerness with which the cousins accepted their fate, even to offering up their very lives for the Lady's sake, left nothing further to be desired.

The sound of heavy, hurried footsteps was heard again, the door was pushed open, and the magistrate strode in.

"Well, that one is finished," he shouted, brushing his hands as if he had just completed a necessary job, and eyeing the prisoners closely to see what effect his scheme was having on them.

"Now watch yourself," he growled, turning to Francisco. "Out with your secret—or else...."

"I cannot tell it to anybody!" said the boy, before the tyrant could finish his threat.

"Is that so! We'll see about that!" And with an exaggerated display of temper and violence poor Francisco was dragged off to share the fate of his brave little sister.

If possible, the magistrate had less success with Francisco than he had encountered with Jacinta. His promises were met with disdainful silence, his threats with baffling indifference.

Finally, it was Lucia's turn to be dragged away to the "chamber of torture." Two failures had now exasperated the puzzled magistrate to the point where evidently no treatment was too merciless for the third recalcitrant victim.

Years later, in her descriptive writings of this trying ordeal, Lucia admits that she thought her last hour had come, but that she had no fear. She had recommended her soul to the all-powerful protection of the beautiful Lady, and was resigned to whatever heaven had in store for her.

At the end of the gruelling inquisition, however, how great was her surprise and her joy to be led to a room where, instead of a boiling kettle of oil, she found her two little companions, safe and sound, although not yet fully recovered from the effects of their terrifying trials.

That night was their second in jail.

The next day on the feast of the Assumption of our Lady, a third assault was made upon their fortitude, and again the children were victorious.

The frustrated official, tired of the unequal contest, began to feel cowardly in the face of such superb moral courage as displayed by the little shepherds. Where, in the name of common sense—he thought—did they ever acquire such strength of opposition?

Oh, if he only knew—if he could only believe, the answer would not be so hard to find! Their strength and resignation could come from no other source than from the Virgin of the Cova, to whom they had given the faithful promise to accept all sufferings, all sacrifices, for the love of God and for her pure and sinless heart.

For the Conversion of Sinners!

Through the grace acquired with the help of the holy Virgin, the children, so fervent in their love for God and the salvation of souls, were consumed by a heavenly thirst—a thirst for souls.

They used every occasion for the satisfaction of this insatiable longing.

On the morning of the day after the first apparition of our Lady they were upon the mountain watching the flock. Jacinta, who had always been the first to propose a game to be played, sat on a large rock, quiet and thoughtful. Noting the unusual attitude of their companion, the other two called out to her:

"Jacinta, why don't you come and play with us?"

"I don't want to play," she answered.

"Why not?"

Slowly the little one replied: "Because I am thinking of what the Lady said yesterday. She told us to say the rosary and to pray for sinners. From now on, we are to say our Hail Marys and Our Fathers without any shortcuts.... But the sacrifices...how shall we make them?"

There followed a few moments of thoughtful silence, while this ponderous question of ascetic science was being settled in their little minds.

"I have it!" cried Francisco, ingeniously. "Let's give our lunch to the sheep! That way we can go fasting!"

They all agreed. For that first day, at least, the manner of sacrificing was decided upon. The Lady would surely be pleased!

Then they began to think of what other sacrifices they could make. One suggestion after the other was adopted, until they had drawn up a program of detailed privations for every day in the week, thus translating into action the injunction of the Virgin that they should offer up many sacrifices for the sins of mankind, and meanwhile proving to an incredulous world the incontrovertible truth of the apparitions and messages of Fatima.

On their way to the pasture, the children would distribute the food they carried for lunch, either among the animals or to some needy persons whom they chanced to meet on the road. Then, for the rest of the day they would undergo a fast as strict as that of a most abstemious saint.

At times, when their hunger became irresistible, they ate pine seed, roots, unripe olives and chiefly unripe acorns, the unpalatable fruit of the holm-oak tree. Jacinta preferred those of the large oak, because they were more bitter than the others. Hearing Lucia say that the acorn of the large oak was entirely too unpalatable, Jacinta explained that that was the precise reason why she preferred them: the more bitter they were, the bigger the penance, and, therefore, the more souls she could save.

Of all the sacrifices they promised to make, the most difficult was to abstain from dancing, an innocent pastime indulged in by all young people of their time, down to the very youngest. This decision was especially trying for little Jacinta, who was especially fond of dancing. But from then on they never again indulged in the innocent frolic.

Their thirst for the conversion of sinners was fully matched by the physical thirst they brought their bodies to endure. It is recorded that they persevered as much as one whole week at a time without taking anything to drink, and in the heat of summer too. One day, up on the mountain, it was particularly hot and depressing. Added to the discomfort of their empty stomachs was the stifling heat of their rocky surroundings. True to their promise to suffer for others, they withstood the agony for several hours. Their throats were parched. Finally, Lucia decided they must get some water, and went to a place nearby to borrow a vessel in which she could carry the refreshment back to her companions.

But when she returned and set the water before them, the thought of the words: "sinners... who offend Jesus"—must have flashed through their minds simultaneously. Guiltily they looked from the tempting liquid to one another. They had but to reach out their hands to end the devouring agony of their bodies. They were not bound by any vow to this torture.

The first to speak was Francisco, "I don't think I want any!"

Lucia was almost offended, having gone to so much trouble to get the water. Sensing her disappointment he added, "I will suffer this for sinners and for the afflicted Jesus!"

Thus encouraged, Jacinta also refused to drink. "So will I make this sacrifice for sinners!"

And so did Lucia.

They then poured the precious water into a small depression in the stony ground for the sheep to drink, and Lucia returned the jug to its owner.

Towards evening, as they sat and listened to a monotonous and almost deafening symphony of frogs and insects, Jacinta, being the youngest and the weakest, began to feel sick from the effects of the long fast. The sounds irritated her.

"What are they singing about!" she said wearily. "My head aches! I can't stand it anymore!"

Her brother intervened tenaciously: "Can't you offer this, too, for sinners?"

"Yes, I will!" said the brave child, and holding her head with her little hands, she said: "Let them fiddle as loud as they wish. It makes no difference to me."

On another occasion, suffering from excessive thirst, Jacinta was on the point of taking a drink from a stagnant pool. Her cousin attempted to prevent her, explaining: "That water will make you ill. Let's go and ask for some pure water!"

"No," replied Jacinta, "I don't want any fresh water. I am making a new kind of sacrifice. Instead of offering my thirst, I will drink this water!"

She was heard to say at times: "The good Lord seems to be content with our sacrifices. I have thirst but have no desire to drink. I want to suffer for His love!"

Evidently they were not yet satisfied with the extent of their sacrifices.

There lived in the village of Aljustrel a vicious woman, who took delight in ridiculing and insulting the children every time she met them, until one day, coming somewhat inebriated out of a tavern, she gave vent to her hatred by beating them.

When the vixen had departed, Jacinta decided to revenge the wicked deed as only saintly souls know how to do. "Let us go and pray to the Virgin," she counseled, "and offer many sacrifices for that poor woman. She sins so much that if she does not mend her life she will go straight to hell!"

Several days later, the children happened to be playing the game of "tag." Just when they were enjoying themselves most, Jacinta suddenly stopped playing and suggested that they cease their play and offer up their amusement as a sacrifice for the usual intention, the conversion of sinners. Thinking no one noticed the action, the little girl raised her hands and eyes toward heaven and exclaimed: "All, O Jesus, for Your love and the conversion of sinners!"

But eyes, other than those of her playmates, had noticed the unusual gesture. Behind the blinds of a house in close vicinity was the woman who had maltreated the shepherds not so long ago, and for whom they had prayed so fervently. She saw the extraordinary action and heard the invocation that rose from the lips of her angelic victim.

Profoundly touched by the scene of a little innocent begging pardon for those who refuse to pray for themselves, she began to recommend her soul to their prayers, that God would forgive her and give her the grace to amend her life.

From then on her life was changed for good.

"Do not forget to pray for sinners who do themselves so much harm!"

How often the children had been admonished with those words, first by the angel, and then by the beautiful Lady, in accents so sweet, but oh, so sad!

How could they forget!

The Never-Ending Fire

The thoughts of "the great sea of fire" which the children witnessed in the third apparition, and of the countless number of souls who suffer there because of their actual and habitual aversion to God, became a sort of obsession. It was a holy obsession—like that of a St. Paul, or a St. Francis Xavier, or a St. Ignatius; of the apostles and missionaries, and all the saints.

The Lady had said that many, many souls go to hell—and they shall burn forever.

Every time Jacinta thought of these words, she was overcome with horror.

"But how?" she would question Lucia. "Will they never leave there? Not even after many years?"

"No, they shall never be released," the more instructed cousin would tell her. "They are condemned for all eternity."

"Eternity!..." Jacinta wrestled with the terrible word, as if to impress it indelibly upon her young mind. She would cup her chin in her little hands and try to ponder the significance of this word so full of meaning. "Do you mean to say they shall never, never get out of hell? Not even after thousands and thousands of years?"

"No, the fire is never-ending; just like heaven, it will never end either."

"And if we pray hard for sinners, and make sacrifices for them, the good Lord will not send them to hell. Isn't it true?" And without waiting for an answer: "What kind of sins do they commit to send them to hell?"

"It's hard to tell!"

Jacinta countered with: "Oh, I feel so sorry for sinners! If I could only make them see what hell is like!"

Then she would hug Lucia and say: "But I am going to heaven! You, Lucia, must stay here for a while longer, and if our Lady permits it, you must tell everybody what hell is, so that they will stay away from sin and not have to go there."

She ended the dialogue with the words that consoled her so much: "How beautiful is the Lady who has promised to take us to herself in heaven. Oh, how beautiful!"

Jacinta did not seem to be a child anymore. Frequently, in the midst of play, she became engrossed in thought, withdrew into her inner consciousness with a faraway look in her eyes: "Hell!... Hell!... Never-ending fire! What a pity that souls should go to everlasting punishment, and burn like fuel in a fire! The poor things! We must pray, pray for them and do more penance."

Sighing and folding her hands in supplication she would repeat the heaven-sent prayer: "O my Jesus, pardon our sins, preserve us from the fire of hell, bring all souls into heaven, especially those most in need of Your mercy!" When she said "all souls," there was such a profound look of gravity and emotion on her features as to remind one of the great thirst of the dying Redeemer on Golgotha.

At times, when the terrifying vision of hell of the third apparition rose up before her like a menacing phantom, she would cry out, "Lucia! Francisco, where are you? Aren't you praying with me? We must pray and pray that souls be saved from damnation. Look! Look.... So many souls are falling into the flames!"

The appalling sight of such souls falling to their eternal doom would cause her to say: "If our Lady would only show sinners the abode of the damned! Once they saw it they would never, never sin and go to such a terrible place. We must ask her to show it to all the people. Then you will see how soon they shall be converted."

As if in ecstasy she would murmur repeatedly: "Oh, how many people are going into hell!... How many people!"

Finding her thus preoccupied, Lucia would enliven her by saying: "Don't fear! You will go to heaven!"

"I know that," she would answer, "but I wish all those people could come with me!"

Francisco, too, was often seized by such troubled thoughts and holy desires, but Lucia, although she had shared the vision of the souls in eternal suffering, as far as we are able to ascertain, never speaks of these things, but we can imagine what her thoughts are, even to this day.

Sacrifice for Sinners

To save as many as possible of these souls in danger of falling into eternal perdition, the shepherds lost very few opportunities for expiation, and no matter how severe the penances were that they imposed upon themselves, they never thought they were doing enough.

Jacinta's mother once gave each a bunch of grapes to eat. They accepted them with evident pleasure, but as soon as they were alone, the youngest exclaimed: "Don't eat them! Let us offer them up as sacrifice for sinners!" She went out of the house with the fruit, intending to distribute it among the neighboring children. When she returned her face was aglow with joy. It happened that two mendicants were passing by at the moment, who gladly accepted the child's gift of charity.

On another occasion, the aunt brought home some delicious figs, and calling the children into the kitchen, set them out for them to eat. "I brought them expressly for you," she said. As they sat about the table and were just ready to eat, Jacinta observed, "We haven't made a sacrifice yet today for the sinners! Let us make one now." And taking the figs in her hand she made the usual "offering."

Out in the pastures, they used to enjoy themselves by searching among the rocks for certain plants. Strange crackling sounds could be made by pressing the leaves between their fingers. By mistake, Jacinta had collected some nettles along with the other plants, and when she pressed on them she winced with pain. But then came an inspiration. She began to press all the harder, ignoring the torture, and with great joy and simplicity she cried out: "Look! Look! Here is another way to do penance!"

Thereafter, they made it a habit to brush their limbs with the nettles, offering the suffering to God for the conversion of sinners.

If, by chance, Jacinta heard anybody using profane or obscene language, she would cover her face, and say, "My God, don't they know they can lose their soul by such conduct? Jesus, I pray for them!"

One morning, passing the Marto house, Lucia went in to bid the family "Good morning." She found Jacinta ill, but when she said she was on her way to attend Mass, Jacinta insisted on accompanying her.

"No, Jacinta, you may not come. Besides, today is not Sunday."

"It makes no difference," the other contended, "I would like to go to Mass, especially for those who miss it on Sundays."

It was shortly after the fourth apparition, in August, 1917. They were taking the sheep to pasture. On the way they found a rope. Lucia picked it up, coiled it on her arm, and carried it along.

They had not gone very far when Lucia exclaimed to her companions, "Do you know, it is painful carrying this rope! What we could do is cut it up, each take a piece and tie it around the waist! Then we could offer the discomfort as a new kind of sacrifice!"

No one objected, so they proceeded to divide the newly found instrument of torture into three parts by rubbing it on the sharp edge of a stone, made several knots in each of the several parts and tied them about their bodies, next to their flesh.

This new form of penance caused them so much physical suffering, day and night, that the youngest, Jacinta, often wept, notwithstanding her love of suffering and Lucia's pleadings to discontinue its use.

What a wonderful spirit of apostolic zeal, love, charity, humility, and self-mortification is evident in these beautiful episodes in the lives of the children of Fatima. So young, simple and tender, yet steeped in the knowledge and grace of God!

In their own eyes they were small, ignorant, and unimportant, but who of us can even begin to measure the grandeur of their souls!

They were always inventing new ways to punish their little bodies out of love for God and His Immaculate Mother, out of pity for ungrateful sinners, and in reparation for a forgetful world.

It is a powerful lesson for a decadent humanity always seeking more and more comforts for its depraved body—oblivious of the needs of its soul—and grudgingly giving its service to the loving Redeemer with the meticulous care that a physician might use in measuring a poisonous medicine.

We set up for ourselves a religion, not of Christ, not of the cross, not of charity, not of perpetual strife against our sinful passions and laziness—but one that will not disturb us too much!

Indeed, to live in the spirit—if not to the very letter—of the commandments of God—we have hundreds of daily occasions for meritorious works for the good of our own souls and the souls of others—poor health, poverty, loss of friendships, deaths. Do we put these misfortunes to work for our eternal salvation—or do we allow them to become a source of sin and rebellion against God and His divine Providence?

It is true that the self-imposed mortifications and sufferings of the three lovers of Mary gradually affected their physical health. As Lucia tells us, little Jacinta was so overcome by the effects of the apparition of July, that the impression it made on her grew to be "all-consuming."

On the evening of September 13, 1917, each of the shepherds, in their bedrooms—empty as a cell but as sacred as a chapel—knelt in prayer to Jesus and Mary. Their countenances were suffused with a light which resembled that heavenly aura that had enshrouded them a few hours earlier in the fifth apparition. Then they began to undress. Reverently they removed the heavy, knotted rope that each carried around the waist. From the very first moment in which they adopted this form of penance, this was the first time, day or night, they had removed it from their body. It was the first sacrifice they were never to complete. And why?

Because on that morning they had been told in the heavenly vision: "The Lord is very much pleased with your sacrifice, but He desires that from now on you shall discard the rope at night, and wear it only in the daytime."

And they obeyed, with that same humble obedience and docile simplicity that Mary loved so well.

An Interview

Of all the afflictions imposed upon the children by others, the worst was the constant flow of visitors to their homes, some well-meaning, others, the majority, mere curiosity-seekers. They came by the thousands, every day and week and month, for the fame of the apparitions had spread far beyond the boundaries of Portugal. The endless talk and questionings in themselves got to be a species of martyrdom for the gentle children and their families.

From the time of the first apparition on, there was also a continual going and coming of vehicles carrying people from every walk of life who desired to see the actual spot where the Virgin appeared and to hear in person from the lips of the "famous children" the "incredible story" of the miracles worked in the Cova. Some were clergymen, entrusted with the duty of ascertaining the true facts of the happenings—a mission which could be accomplished only by long and tedious interviews. Others came to have the children recommend them in their prayers, to ask special favors from heaven, even asking them to say the rosary with them, that thus their prayers might be more readily answered.

Lucia writes: "Whenever we grew weary of answering the same questions over and over, we excused ourselves with some pretext for leaving and went into hiding. Nevertheless, the insistence of the visitors was so great, that we made an effort, and no small one, to satisfy them when possible. When evening came we were exhausted, but sometimes the interrogations went on into the night. Often the crowds were so large that those who could not be admitted through the day waited all night to take their turn at admittance on the following morning."

The parish priest of Fatima, speaking in the month of October, 1917, declared "that the number of visitors has become so great, that it is a miracle in itself that the children do not succumb to the ordeal."

Among the visitors, there was one, however, who came with proper spirit and with the best intentions: a pious, learned priest, and professor of Theology in the Patriarchal Seminary in Lisbon. We should like to identify him, for the present, as the "historian" of the events of Fatima. In his first visit to the Dos Santos home on September 14, 1917, he introduced himself under the pseudonym of "Viscount of Montelo," and by this quaint name by which he attached himself to the story, and by the gentleness of his manners, he soon won the sympathy and respect of all concerned.

He asked to speak with the shepherds. Lucia was out with some other members of the family, harvesting, but the mother, Mary-Rose, had her summoned at once.

Soon, Francisco and Jacinta were sent for, and when they had learned that an important personage was at Lucia's house and wished to see them, they came in a hurry.

Jacinta was the first to appear.

Sketching the little girl with a few concise phrases the "Viscount" began to take notes: "Seven years old—sufficiently developed for her age—features regular—color, dark—modestly dressed, skirt reaching to ankles."

The presence of the distinguished gentleman, with pencil and paper in hand, and ready to write down whatever answers she might give to his questions so embarrassed the little one that she became almost speechless—she who had hitherto been so talkative and brave.

Fortunately, Francisco arrived in the meantime, and his presence gave her encouragement.

Without much ado, his hat on his head, and seating himself before the clerical reporter without asking anyone's permission, Francisco assumed an attitude of willingness to answer anything the strange, but amiable looking priest might ask of him.

We should like to give a verbatim account of the highlights of this interesting interview, following closely that most authoritative book *Le Meraviglie di Fatima*, written by Rev. L. Gonzaga Da Fonseca, S.J., Professor at the Pontifical Biblical Institute in Rome.

The interrogations serve both as a historical complement to and as a confirmation of the famous apparitions.

"Francis, who was it you saw in these few months in the Cova da Iria?" asked the Viscount precipitately.

The boy answered promptly: "The Virgin!"

"Where did she appear?"

"At the top of a holm-oak tree."

"Did she come unexpectedly or did she approach gradually from some certain direction?"

"I saw her come from the direction of the rising sun, and she stopped when she reached the tree."

"Did she come slowly or rapidly?"

"She always came rapidly."

"Could you hear what she said to Lucia?"

"No. I could hear nothing."

"Did you at any time speak to the Lady, or she to you?"

"No. I never said anything. She spoke only to Lucia."

"At whom did she look? At all three of you, or only at Lucia?"

"At all of us, but mostly at Lucia."

"And, hitherto, had she smiled or wept?"

"Neither the one nor the other. She was always serious."

"How was she dressed?"

"She wore a long gown, and over that a cloak that covered her from head to foot."

"What was the color of the gown and cloak?"

"They were white, with golden edges."

"And what position did she assume?"

"Like that of one who prays. She had her hands joined on her breast."

"Did she have anything in her hands?"

"Over the palm and back of the right hand hung a rosary, down to the end of her gown."

"Did she wear anything in her ears?"

"Her ears could not be seen, because the cloak covered them."

"What was the color of the beads of the rosary?"

"They were white, too."

"Was the Lady beautiful?"

"Oh, yes!"

"More beautiful than that girl you see there?" —pointing to a girl outside in the yard.

"Oh yes, much more!"

"But there are many ladies more beautiful than that girl!"

"The Lady was more beautiful than anybody I have ever seen."

Jacinta was not present at her brother's interview. Confused and embarrassed, she had run away to play with the other children. Being summoned a second time, she conquered her backwardness, and answered every question with coolness and exactness, confirming fully every assertion that her brother had made.

"Whether she had seen the Lady?"..."Certainly!—She had seen her—in the Cova—at the direction of the rising sun!"

"And how was she dressed?"..."In a white gown, edged in gold—and with a white cloak over her head!"

"Beautiful?"..."Most beautiful person in the world!—but she always seemed so sad!"

"Color of her hair?"..."She could not see her hair—it was hidden by the cloak."

"Earrings?"..."She could not see her ears."

"How did she hold her hands?"..."Her hands were joined just above her breast, the fingers pointing upward."

"Was the rosary on the right hand or on the left?"

"On the right hand," she promptly replied, but as this was questioned, wishing to avoid contradictions, she became nervous and uncertain, since it is not so easy for young children to designate as to the right or left of themselves the corresponding hand of another person facing them.

"What was it the Lady so insistently demanded from Lucia?"

"To recite the rosary every day."

"And do you recite it?"

"Yes, every day—with Francisco and Lucia!"

About a half hour later Lucia arrived, coming in from the vineyard, in obedience to the mother's summons.

"Tall, well developed, robust, polite, natural in her manners, without the slightest trace of affectation." The reporter, thus far, was not deceived in the children.

Although averse to questioning, Lucia was now docile and obliging, revealing no sign of vanity.

"Is it really true that our Lady appeared to you in a place called the Cova da Iria?"

"Yes, it is true."

"How many times did she appear to you?"

"Five times; once a month."

"On what day of the month?"

"Always on the 13th, except in August, when I was arrested and taken away by the Administrator. In that month I saw her a few days later at Valinhos."

"People say that the Virgin appeared to you a year ago, also. Is that true?"

"No, it is not. Neither last year, nor this year before the month of May. I never said she did, because it is not so."

"From which direction did the Virgin approach you? From the east?"

"That I could not say. I did not notice that she came from any particular direction." This answer is remarkable in that it does not confirm the testimony given by the other two children. With scrupulous veracity, Lucia tried later on to explain that the lights that always heralded the immediate approach of the Virgin "were not exactly flashes, but more like a reflection of a light that approached gradually. In this light we saw the Lady when it came to rest above the little tree. The fact that we could not explain it, or that I seem to avoid the question, is because we said we sometimes noticed her coming, and sometimes we didn't. When we say we noticed her approach, we refer to the light that came toward us, which is the same thing, practically, as saying the Lady approached us; and when we said we didn't see her coming, we meant that we saw her only when she had appeared over the tree. Therefore, she appeared—she didn't arrive. And whenever she left, she went in the direction of the sunrise."

"How long would she stay? For a long or short time?"

"Just for a short time."

"Enough time to say a Hail Mary and an Our Father—or more?"

"Oh, more! Much more! But not always for the same length of time. Not enough, perhaps, even to say a rosary."

"When you first saw her, were you not afraid?"

"Yes, and I wanted to run away, with Francisco and Jacinta. But she told us not to fear, that she would not harm us." (Later, Lucia, as a nun, explains this fear more fully: "The fear we felt was caused, not so much by the Virgin, as by what had seemed to be an imminent storm. The Virgin's appearance was not terrifying, but rather surprising.")

"How was she dressed?"

"In a white gown that fell almost to her feet, and over the gown she wore a cloak, which also was white, but longer than the gown since it covered her head, too." (We hope the reader will kindly pardon another interruption in the account of the interview, so that we may record an interesting observation made by Lucia later on in the convent. "In some images that I have seen, depicting Our Lady of Fatima, she seems to have two cloaks. If I were an artist—although I know I could never show her to be near so beautiful as she really was, for that is just as impossible to do as it is for me to try to express it in words—I would show a simple gown of purest white, and a single cloak reaching down to the hem of the gown. And if I could not portray the light and the ineffable beauty that glorified her, I would eliminate all ornamentation except the gold edging of the cloak. These marginal gold threads were outstandingly brilliant. Some images are not at all like the original, which I cannot describe any better.")

"Was her apparel ornamented in any way?"

Lucia responded: "Two gold cords extended from her neck down to about the middle of her body, and there they were united in a tassel of pure gold."

"Did she wear a ribbon of any kind?"

"None."

"Nor earrings?"

"Yes, small, circular earrings." Lucia modified this statement by saying: "I did not see the earrings. But with the light flashing through the gold mesh on the edge of the cloak, I imagined several times as I looked where the cloak fell from the head onto the shoulders, that the Lady wore earrings."

"In which hand did she hold the rosary?"

"In the right hand."

"Was it a whole rosary, or only a part?"

"I did not notice that."

"Did it end in a cross?"

"Yes, in a white cross. The beads and chain were also white."

"Didn't you ask her who she was?"

"Yes, but she said she would tell me her name on the 13th of October."

"And did you ask her where she came from?"

"Yes, and she said, 'from heaven'!"

"Did she ever smile, or was she sad?"

"I never saw her smile—she always seemed sad!"

"Did she exhort you to say certain prayers?"

"Yes, she told us to pray the rosary in honor of our Lady and for the peace of the world."

"Did she instruct you to say any other prayers?"

"Yes, the prayer that we are to recite after every mystery of the rosary."

"Can you recite it from memory?"

"Yes."

"Say it for me."

"O Jesus, grant us pardon for our sins, preserve us from the fire of hell, and bring into heaven all souls, especially those most in need of Your mercy."

"Did she express the desire to have large crowds of people attend the apparitions on the 13th of every month?"

"She did not say anything concerning that."

"Is it true that she confided a secret to you with the express command to tell it to no one?"

"Yes, that is true."

"Only to you, or to your companions also?"

"To each one of us."

"Are you not permitted to tell it even to your confessor?" Such questions as this last one always perplexed Lucia. And she never knew what answer to make. It was indiscreet of the reporter, to say the least, so he proceeded to the next one.

"It has been said that to put an end to the annoying demands of the Administrator, who sought to extract the secret from you, you told him a story that was not true, in order to deceive him, and that you boasted later on of having tricked him. Is that true?"

"That is an untruth. The Administrator did demand that I reveal the secret, but I refused to tell him, since I was forbidden to do so. Instead of giving him the secret, I told him everything the Lady had said. Perhaps the Administrator took that for the secret itself. I had no intention of deceiving him."

"Did the Lady tell you that you must learn to read?"

"Yes, when she appeared the second time."

"But if she told you that you were to be taken into heaven by the 13th of October, what would be the use of learning to read?"

"It is not true that she said that, and I never said she did."

"On the 13th of October, will the Lady come alone?"

"She will come with St. Joseph and the Infant Jesus."

"Did she make any other revelations?"

"She said she would work a great miracle to prove to everybody that she had appeared to us."

"For what reason did you often lower your eyes and cease looking at the Lady?"

"Because the vision blinded my eyes."

"Are you glad that you saw the Lady?"

"Very much so—indeed!"

The interlocutor appeared content, if not too fully satisfied with the interview. The shepherds had understood very well what they said, and what they were supposed to tell. He went away to report the outcome of his first interview to those who had sent him.

Further Questioning

On October 11, 1917, the Viscount of Montelo was journeying toward Fatima, but decided, for the sake of convenience, to stay a while in Villanova de Ourem, and to pay a visit to a highly respected family called Goncalves, where he hoped to obtain a dispassionate and trustworthy appraisal of the story of the three shepherds along with a history of their family connections.

The results were very satisfactory. He writes: "The parents of Francisco and Jacinta are a wholesome and God-fearing couple, respected by everybody and held in high esteem. The father is considered one of the most honest men of the village, and therefore not prone to deceit. Lucia's father is a good man, not overly assiduous in his religious duties but, nevertheless, not a man of evil propensities. Her mother is an honorable woman, religious, and energetic."

"And what do the people think of the children's assertions?" he asked.

"In the beginning nobody believed them; but now, for the most part, they believe the children are telling the truth. On the days of the appointed apparitions some very extraordinary things do happen, and there are some who have actually witnessed them. The wonders are manifold. In August, nearly everyone present saw them. A cloud descended on the holm-oak tree. There was no dust up there. In fact, the cloud darkened the atmosphere bewilderingly. The intensity of the sun's rays was diminished...a thunderous sound was heard in the events of July and August."

"Is there any suspicion, that, perhaps, somebody has induced the children to put on a show?"

"No, that is not very likely."

"Do many people come from afar to see and speak with the children?"

"Very many, from all parts."

"Do the children accept any money if it is offered to them?"

"They have accepted some trivial presents, but only under great pressure, and unwillingly."

"Are the parents poor?"

"Not extremely poor; comparatively well-to-do. And if Lucia's father were not so indifferent about cultivating his land, they would enjoy many more comforts."

"What does Lucia do during the apparitions?"

"She recites the rosary. And when she deals directly with the vision she speaks out loud."

"Is the place of the apparitions visited very much by both devout and curious people?"

"Very much so, especially on Sundays. They come from far and near. Many are from the neighboring parishes."

"How do the people behave at the place of the apparitions?"

"They recite the rosary, and sing popular hymns in honor of our Lady."

With this information in his possession, the Viscount set out for Aljustrel, and went directly to the home of Lucia. The mother, Mary-Rose, recognized him, received him with high respect and honor, and condescendingly submitted herself to his questioning:

"How did you come to find out that the Lady appeared to your daughter? Did she herself inform you?"

"I learned of it through the family of the other two children, because Lucia, fearful of reproval, had counseled her cousins to say nothing about it, but upon questioning her, she told the whole story of what she had seen."

"Did you allow her to go freely to the Cova on the 13th of each month?"

"I never stopped her from going."

"How were the children dressed when they went there?"

"The first time they were rather poorly dressed as befits a shepherd, but after that, they dressed in bright clothes, with a white headdress also."

"When the children were taken away and held by the Administrator, did anybody go to their assistance?"

"A brother of Francisco and Jacinta went to their aid but could not effect their release, because they were confined in the Administrator's own house."

"Have many people come usually to see your daughter?"

"We have visitors every day, without let-up."

As the questioning went on the mother regarded the visitor with an eye of perplexity mixed with a strong desire to read in his countenance the answer to the enigma she thought she would never be able to solve. Had the Blessed Virgin really blessed her daughter with the vision of her own celestial person—or was it, after all, a horrible hallucination? Her heart was heavy, indeed.

"Let us hope," the sorrowing woman said finally, as tears welled up in her eyes, "let us hope, that in one way or another, something will soon turn up to settle the question, clearly and conclusively," thus demonstrating the rectitude and the resignation of her motherly heart, anxious for one thing only—the recognition of divine truth.

The Viscount smiled in understanding sympathy—for to hear such words had been precisely one of the main objects of his visit.

Then he turned to Lucia. "Well, Lucia, now it's your turn!" And the dialogue began to concern itself about the miracle which was actually scheduled to take place within two days, that is, on the 13th of October.

"Have you no fear of the people's derision if nothing extraordinary happens on that day?"

"I do not fear anything, since the Lady has given her promise."

"What are the signs to be, that are to give credit to the apparition?"

"She said a miracle is to happen."

"When did she say that?"

"She told me several times."

"Do you feel within you any special attraction toward the Cova on the 13th of the month?"

"Yes, I have a great desire to go there, and would feel sad if I could not go."

"Have you ever seen the Lady make the sign of the cross, pray, or use the beads of the rosary?"

"No, I never noticed her doing any of those things."

"But she told you to pray?"

"Many times."

"Are you certain on what spot the Lady desires that a chapel be built in her honor?"

"Not the exact spot, but I think she wants it to be in the Cova."

"Have you ever seen, as some people claim to have seen, roses come or stars detaching themselves from the Lady's clothing?"

"No, I never saw any stars or other extraordinary thing about her."

"Have you been conscious of any loud or thunderous sounds, or earthquakes?"

"Never!"

"Can you read?"

"No, sir."

"Are you learning to read?"

The girl was constrained to answer: "No."

"Then why do you not heed the command of the Lady?"

Lucia was silent. She did not wish to blame her mother, who had denied her permission to attend school. In fact, her family had attributed it to vanity on Lucia's part when she had expressed a desire for such learning. In those days, it was customary in Fatima and other places in the interior to grant this privilege to boys only.

"When you tell the crowds to kneel and pray —is that an order that comes from the Lady?"

"The Lady never gave such an order. I am the one who desires it."

"Do you always kneel when she appears?"

"There are times when I stand."

"When she speaks—is her voice sweet and pleasant?"

"Yes."

"About what age does she appear to be?"

"About fifteen."

"Does the cloak cover her in front?"

"No. The front is uncovered by the cloak."

"Could you describe the splendor that surrounds her?"

"It is more beautiful and more dazzling than the sun!"

"Did she ever salute you with her head or hand?"

"Never."

"She never smiles?"

"No, never!"

"When you see her, are you ever conscious of the conversation, the noise, the cries of the bystanders?"

"I hear none of it whatever."

And thus the questioning and answering went on, cleverly and categorically. Lucia knew her business.

"Let us hear from you, now, Jacinta! Have you, too, a secret, or is Lucia the only one who is so privileged?"

"I have one, too."

"And when did you get it?"

"At the second visit—or, on the feast-day of St. Anthony."

"Is the secret such, perhaps, that you shall some day be rich?"

"No."

"Or that you shall be happy and content?"

"Yes, for all three of us."

"That you shall go to heaven?"

"No."

"Are you not permitted to tell me?"

"No, I am not permitted."

"Why?"

"Because the Lady told me to tell no one."

"If people got to know it, would it, perhaps, be to their sorrow?"

"Yes."

"How did the Lady hold her hands?"

"She held them high. Often she would turn the palms toward heaven."

"Did she have a halo around her head?"

"Yes."

"Could you see her face very plainly?"

"No, I couldn't, because the light hurt my eyes."

"Did you always hear distinctly what the Lady said?"

"The last time I couldn't hear her very well, because the people made so much noise!"

Finally, Francisco was interrogated for the second time by the Viscount, but his answers never deviated from those previously given.

The slightest doubt, if any had existed, that the children had studied and memorized their answers was now dissipated, like snow in the warm rays of the sun.

But how are we to account for the firmness of their statements—the identity of their testimony in a multiplicity of questionings, not only of the gentle Viscount, but especially of the terrifying Administrator and his henchmen? It could not have been from an exalted imagination. They were illiterate, and had not proper background for such fiction. Sick minds?—They were normal, healthy children. To put on a show?—For whom? They were ridiculed and jeered and severely punished by their families, friends, and even by strangers. Priestcraft?—No. Such a charge would be ridiculous. The parish priest refused to be interested, and was even accused by the people of being hostile to the children. We are told by Lucia when the demands of the parishioners became too pressing, he fled the parish rather that assume any responsibility in connection with the apparitions. Was it for money?—Impossible. The families of the children never received a penny from the charity of the faithful, in fact, as we have seen, Lucia's family was made more impoverished than before by the destruction of their property in the Cova.

We read in the pastoral letter of 1930, dealing with the cult of Our Lady of Fatima: "There is no evidence of self-interest or vanity in the parents of the children. When they decided to take over the direction of the doings of Fatima, which they relinquished entirely, they turned over to us all the money and objects of value that had been deposited at the site of the apparitions."

Furthermore, in the years following the events of Fatima (Lucia's mother, Mary-Rose, lived until 1942), there was no noticeable change in the mode of living of the two families. The parents of Francisco and Jacinta, modest and retired, were happy or the blessings that have come to the world from Mary through their children.

The Sunset of
the Day of Days

Our next contact with that venerable figure, the Viscount of Montelo, is when he emerged, on the afternoon of that day of days in Fatima, from a milling, frantic crowd of thousands of people who sought approach to the shepherds of Aljustrel in the moment of their climactic popular triumph, immediately after the final appearance of our Lady.

The tribute of the delirious people proved almost fatal for poor little Jacinta who was crushed and nearly suffocated in the surging crowds, saved only by being hoisted onto the shoulders of some thoughtful member of the throng. So, too, was Lucia carried away, her body bobbing up and down above a veritable sea of faces. Once, when her momentary protector, unable to feel his way, stumbled and fell over a pile of stones, his living burden fell onto still another's shoulders, so tight was the frenzied wall of humanity that surrounded her.

At last, tattered and bruised and half conscious, the children arrived at home. The crowds had centered their "affections" more on Lucia than on the younger children. Her clothes were cut and torn, her headdress was snatched away, and even her beautiful long tresses were clipped off, so that when she got home "her hair was just as short as that of Francisco."

All afternoon and into the night, the indiscreet, but jubilant people, welled about the house, desiring to see, to hear, to touch the privileged little shepherds, and seeking to learn what the Lady had said in the apparition.

There was one person, however, who was a welcome inquisitor this day in the house of Marto: he, who, on his first visit, had won the respect and the confidence of the children and of their families. They were genuinely glad to see him. Perhaps we, too, should be thankful to this worthy person for his persistent efforts to complete his investigation while the impressions of the day's happenings were still fresh in the little children's minds, even to the disturbance and distraction of the blissful emotions of his hosts on this memorable date.

Speaking first to Lucia, who, for the present, was with her cousins, he questioned her: "Is it true that the Lady appeared today in the Cova da Iria?"

"Yes."

"Was she dressed as usual?"

"Yes, she was dressed the same as before."

"Is it true that St. Joseph and the Infant Jesus also appeared?"

"Yes, it is true."

"Did anyone else appear to you?"

"Yes, our Lord appeared in the attitude of blessing the people, and the Virgin appeared in two different forms."

"What is meant by the words 'in two forms'?"

"I mean that she appeared as the Mother of Sorrows, but without the sword through her heart, and again as—I may not be describing it exactly— as resembling Our Lady of Mt. Carmel."

"Did these two visions occur at the same time?"

"No, I saw first of all Our Lady of the Rosary, St. Joseph and the Infant Jesus; then our Lord,

alone; after that, the Mother of Sorrows, and last-
ly, Our Lady of Mt. Carmel."

"Was the Infant standing or in the arms of
St. Joseph?"

"He was in the arms of St. Joseph."

"Was the Infant rather big?"

"No, very young."

"About what age did He appear to be?"

"About a year old."

"Did you see all this at the oak tree?"

"No. They appeared close to the sun, after the
Lady had gone from the oak tree."

"Was our Lord in a standing position?"

"I could see only the upper half of His body."

"How long did the apparition last at the oak
tree? About as long as it would take to say a
rosary?"

"Not quite."

"And the figures you saw by the sun, did they
remain very long?"

"No, only for a short time."

"Has the Lady told you her name?"

"Yes, she told me that she is Our Lady of the
Rosary."

"Did you ask her what it is she desires?"

"Yes, I asked her."

"And what was her answer?"

"She said we must mend our lives, and not
add to the offenses that are now being committed
against our Lord; to say the rosary, and to ask pardon for our sins."

"Nothing else?"

"She also expressed the desire to have a chapel
built in the Cova da Iria."

"And where is the money to be gotten to build such a chapel?"

"I suppose with the money that people leave there."

"Did she say anything about our soldiers who died in the war?"

"Not a thing."

"Was it she who told you to direct the attention of the crowd to the sun?"

"No, she did not."

"Does she wish for the people to do penance?"

"Yes."

"Did she use the word 'penance'?"

"No, she said to recite the rosary, to mend our lives, to ask pardon of our Lord for our sins. She didn't use the word 'penance.' "

"When did you first notice the prodigy of the sun?—When the lady had gone?"

"Yes."

"Did you see her approaching you?"

"Yes."

"From what direction?"

"From the east."

"The same as before?"

"I never gave it any attention before."

"Did you see her depart?"

"Yes."

"Toward which direction?"

"Toward the east."

"When she left, did she just recede, or did she turn her back to the people?"

"She turned her back to the people."

"Did her departure take up much time?"

"No, just a few moments."

"Was there a brightness about her?"

"She always came in a dazzling light; but this time it was especially overpowering. Several times I had to rub my eyes."

"Do you think she shall appear again?"

"I don't expect to see her again. She said nothing about coming again."

"Do you intend to go up to the Cova on the 13th of next month?"

"No, sir."

"Will the Lady work no more miracles? Will she not heal the sick?"

"I don't know that."

"Did you not make any request?"

"I told her today that I had several favors to ask of her. She said some would be granted, others would not."

"Did she say when they would be granted?"

"No."

"Under what title is the chapel in the Cova to be erected?"

"She said today that she is the Lady of the Holy Rosary."

"Does she wish, perhaps, that people should come here from far and near?"

"She did not give such an order."

"Did you see any wonders in the sun?"

"Yes, I saw it whirling."

"Did any other wonders occur at the oak tree?"

"I didn't notice any."

"When did the Lady appear most beautiful to you? Today—or on the other days?"

"She always has the same beauty."

"What was the color of her dress when she appeared near the sun?"

"The cloak was blue, and the gown was white."

"And the color of the robes of St. Joseph, and of the Infant Jesus?"

"Their robes were red."

"When did you ask the Lady what should be done to convince people of the apparitions?"

"The first time was in June, I think; since then, many times."

The next one to be interrogated was Jacinta.

"Besides the Lady, who else appeared today in the Cova?"

"I saw St. Joseph, and the Infant Jesus."

"Where did they appear?"

"I saw them alongside the sun."

"Was the Infant Jesus on the right, or the left side of St. Joseph?"

"He was on the right side."

"Standing, or in St. Joseph's arms?"

"Standing."

"Could you see the right arm of St. Joseph?"

"No."

"How tall did the Infant seem to be?"

"He did not even reach up to St. Joseph's girdle."

"About how old did the Infant appear to be?"

Jacinta had difficulty in judging the age, but she explained it in her own childish fashion, saying: "He was about the size of Deolinda das Neves"—a child of the neighborhood, and about two years of age.

"What did the Lady speak about?"

"She said we should say the rosary every day; better our lives; and not offend our Lord so much; and to build a chapel in the Cova."

"Did you hear her say those words, or did Lucia tell them to you?"

"I heard her telling it myself."

"From which direction did she come?"

"From where the sun rises."

"And when she left?"

"Toward sunrise."

"Did she face the people as she disappeared?"

"No. Her face was turned away from the people."

"Did she tell you to come again to the Cova?"

"She said long ago that today would be the last. And she said it again today that this was the last time."

"Did she say nothing else?"

"She said that the rosary should be said every day to the Lady of the Rosary."

"Did she say where the rosary should be recited?"

"She didn't say where."

"Did she suggest that it be recited in Church?"

"No, she didn't."

"Where do you like best to recite the rosary— in your home or in the Cova da Iria?"

"In the Cova."

"Why?"

"Oh, just because...!"

"With what money did the Lady say the chapel is to be built?"

"She just said the chapel is to be built—she didn't say anything about money."

"Did you notice the sun today?"

"Yes."

"And how did it look?"

"It looked red, and green, and all colors—and I saw it spin around."

"Did you hear Lucia telling the people to look at the sun?"

"I heard her, yes. Lucia said it out loud, for them to look at the sun. It was spinning then, already."

"Was it an order from the Lady, that they should look at the sun?"

"No, she didn't order it."

Francisco's testimony corroborated the statements of the other two. He too had seen the Lady —but had heard nothing she said. She was dressed in white—held a rosary in her hand. He too had seen St. Joseph and the Infant Jesus.

To see whether his and Jacinta's testimony coincided, the Viscount asked him:

"Was the Infant sitting on St. Joseph's arm, or was He standing?"

"He was standing beside St. Joseph."

"Was He big or little?"

"Very little."

"Like Deolinda das Neves—perhaps?"

"Just the same size!"

"How did the Lady hold her hands?"

"They were joined."

"Did you see her only at the oak tree, or near the sun, also?"

"I saw her near the sun, too."

"Which was the brightest, the sun or the Lady?"

"The face of the Lady was brighter."

"Did you hear her say anything?"

"I didn't hear anything she said."

"Who told you the secret? The Lady?"

"No—Lucia!"

"Could you tell it to me?"

"No. I am not permitted."

"You do not wish to tell me because you are afraid of Lucia? That she might punish you, perhaps?"

"Oh, no!"

"Well, then, why not tell me? Would it be sinful to tell me?"

"Maybe!"

"Is the secret something that promises good for your soul, and for the soul of Lucia and Jacinta?"

"Yes."

"And perhaps for the good of the soul of the parish priest?"

"That I could not say."

"Would it cause anybody sadness if it were to be revealed?"

"Yes."

"From which direction did the Lady come when she appeared?"

"From the east."

"And did she disappear in the same direction?"

"Yes."

"Backwards?"

"No, she turned around."

"Fast or slowly?"

"Slowly."

"Did she walk, like we do?"

"She didn't walk; she moved away, slowly, without moving her feet."

"When did she appear to be more beautiful?—This time, or before?"

"She never changes in her beauty."

"Did you, too, see the wonders in the sun?"

"Yes, I saw the sun when it whirled around. It looked like a wheel of fire."

"Did this miracle occur before or after she disappeared?"

"Right after she had disappeared."

"And the miracle began suddenly?"

"Yes."

"What colors did you see in the sun?"

"I saw beautiful colors: blue, yellow, and all kinds."

On that eventful day of October 13, 1917, as we can see, the shepherds had no time to invent their stories, to exchange ideas, or to make any plans to effect a coincidence in their statements. Promptly and sincerely they told what each had seen or heard, with no embellishment, and without adding or subtracting one bit of truth.

Greatly impressed by the firmness and conviction of the children, the Viscount of Montelo bade farewell to the children and their relatives, who had been so kind and patient and condescending with him. His mind and heart were convinced: "No, this is no mere invention; nor can it possibly be hallucination."

Then and there he decided to write the story of Fatima—to throw into the face of a sophisticated and incredulous world a formidable and indisputable document that would be as truthful and radiant as the souls of the little children themselves.

Thus he planned, as he departed from the little village, soon to have its fame spread over the whole world. It was evening. Lights began to appear in the windows of the villagers, symbolic of the celestial lights of Fatima that shall nevermore be extinguished.

The Eucharist
and the Pope

It is a source of perpetual wonder and admiration to consider the various devotions of the little children, from which there emerged such a love and attachment to Jesus in the Blessed Sacrament, and to the Holy Father, to the "sweet Christ on earth." Their tears and pleadings were many for the unfaithfulness and treachery of mankind because of which the passion of the Son of Man is renewed in the Church down through the centuries.

Following the expressed desire of our Lady, Lucia began to attend school shortly after the last apparition. So too did the cousins, whose parents were prevailed upon by interested authorities and friends to allow them to accompany Lucia.

Arriving at the school, they never failed to enter the nearby church to spend a few moments in adoration of the Blessed Sacrament. They would kneel before the little wooden tabernacle in the same attitude of heavenly entrancement that engrossed them in the Cova at the feet of the beautiful Lady.

Jesus was hidden on the altar, under the veil of the Sacrament, and when it came time to interrupt their adoration to go to school, Francisco would sometimes say to Lucia: "You go to school! I am going to stay here with the hidden Jesus. What good will it do me to learn to read! In a short while I shall be in heaven! Come in and call for me on your way home!" And when Lucia would return, she would find him in the same place, near the altar, his hands folded, and his eyes fixed on the tabernacle.

Several months later Francisco's prediction began to be verified. His fatal sickness had come upon him. On the streets of Fatima, accompanied by Lucia, he made his way with difficulty toward that pulsing heart—center of the blessed little village, the altar of God.

"My head hurts!... I think I am going to fall down!" His weakness was extreme.

"Let us go back home!" said Lucia.

"No! No! I love to be in church while you go to class!"

Later on, when the ravages of his sickness confined him to his home, his only sorrow was that he could no longer make his visits to Jesus in the Sacrament. He would say to Lucia: "Go into the church and tell Jesus everything for me!"

Love for the divine Prisoner had also become a consuming passion in the heart of his little sister Jacinta. Nothing pleased her more than to spend her time in loving, silent homage before her Eucharistic Lord. "I love it here," she would say, "and I have so much to tell Him!"

One day, Lucia offered her a beautiful little picture of the Sacred Heart. She took it, examined and contemplated it for awhile, then observed with the discernment of one who, in an infusion of supernatural grace, had looked into the face of the Eternal: "It is ugly! It does not resemble our Lord at all, who is so beautiful! But I will keep it. After all, it is He!"

She carried the precious object around with her, and placed it under her pillow at night. She would impress upon it, from time to time, symbols of her innocent affection: "I kiss this heart, which is the dearest of all things to me—the heart which beats in the Sacred Host. I would like also a picture of the heart of Mary, to have the two hearts together."

Interiorly illuminated, and instructed by two zealous priests as to the identity of the Holy Father, designated by the Virgin as in need of so many prayers, the shepherds actually stormed heaven with their pleadings that the Great Shepherd of the entire Church might obtain strength and courage to carry the heavy burden of his office.

Their heartfelt cries for supernatural aid ascended to the throne of Mercy at the conclusion of all their prayers: "...and for the Holy Father!" They began to say three "Hail Marys" after every recitation of the rosary for the sorely tried Pontiff —revealed to them in vision, but who was so far, far away in another land.

Since that day when Jacinta was permitted in a sweeping panoramic vision to behold the bloody ravages of war, the famishing, wandering peoples, and the Holy Father kneeling in tearful prayer, his great house surrounded by mobs bent on his destruction, they had taken the Great Pastor to their hearts, and never forgot him in their prayers.

They often expressed a fervent desire to see the Vicar of Christ in person. "We see so many people coming to visit us, but oh, how glad we would be to see him. But that can never be!"

This loyalty and affection was once severely tested. Lucia tells us: "We were imbued with such a great love for the Holy Father, that when the pastor one day came to my mother and told her that I might be sent to Rome to be interrogated, I clapped my hands and said to my little cousins, 'O joy! I shall see the Pope!' Tearfully they answered: 'We shall never see him, perhaps, but we will be patient; and even this we will offer up as a new sacrifice for his sake.' "

In a further revelation of the sympathetic love of the children for the suffering Leader of Christendom, Lucia wrote in a recent letter to the Bishop of Leiria: "Jacinta was deeply concerned with everything pertaining to the 'Secret'; and in her boundless love for the Pontiff and for sinners she would often exclaim: 'What a pity for the poor Pope!... I feel so sorry for sinners also!' Interpreting these sentiments of Jacinta, I formulated this fervent, ardent prayer: 'Would to God that her recommendation of the Head of the Church and of all the priests could be shared and practiced in every corner of the earth!' "

Let us imitate these virtues of the pious shepherds when we contemplate the silent sufferings of the Holy Father; the indifference and the desertions of once loyal, Catholic nations. Let us echo the cries that are poured forth to a merciful heaven by the pilgrims in the Cova da Iria:

"Our Lady of Fatima, bless our Pontiff!"

Grateful Hearts

A visiting priest one day told Lucia that she should never forget to thank God often for the singular graces He had conferred upon her. She was profoundly impressed by this priestly advice, and having decided to formulate a prayer of gratitude to be included in her daily devotions, she communicated her aspirations to her little companions.

Heaven loves a grateful heart, and in consequence additional favors were showered upon these pure souls. Among these was the gift of obtaining many favors for the people at large, material as well as spiritual ones. They had become famous throughout the land, and many, distressed in body and soul, sought their intercession with God and His holy Mother.

She who had taught them how to pray, who had come down from heaven to talk to them, and to reveal herself to them in all her celestial beauty —how could she fail to hear their prayers!

The tearful supplications of Lucia once saved her mother's life in a mortal illness.

Jacinta was especially gifted in this respect. Lucia has revealed several happenings in proof of this.

One day a sorrowing woman came to Jacinta weeping, and throwing herself on her knees before the girl, she begged her to obtain from our Lady the grace of a cure for a horrible sickness that afflicted her. The child was so moved by the sight of a

woman kneeling to her that she tremblingly hastened to assist her to her feet. Jacinta's little
strength was unavailing, so she herself knelt beside
the distressed woman, and told her to pray. Together they prayed three "Hail Marys" and when
they had risen to their feet, Jacinta assured the
humble woman that the Virgin would help her.

Keeping the incident in mind, the little saint
prayed perseveringly for the woman, who shortly
afterwards returned to give joyful thanks to the
Mother of God for the restoration of her health.

A soldier about to depart for the front line of
battle came to Jacinta in despair, begging her to
pray for his intention, because he was leaving a
sickly wife and three small children at home. Jacinta invited him to say a rosary with her. He joyfully accepted and they prayed together. Then she
said: "Our Lady is good! I know she will help you!"
From that day on the soldier's misfortune was
never forgotten in her daily prayers.

Several months later he came back, accompanied by his wife and children, to thank the child
and God's Blessed Mother for favors received. On
the eve of his scheduled departure to the battlefields he was stricken with a sudden and violent
fever than rendered him unfit for military service,
and his wife, too, was instantaneously cured of her
sickness. Truly—a double miracle had been the reward of the privileged child of Mary.

A family, closely related to that of the children, had a son, who was similar to the prodigal in
the Gospel and had left his home for parts
unknown, but without previous warning of his intentions. The desolate mother hastened to pour out

her grief to Jacinta. "Please pray for him, Jacinta, and ask the Mother of God to bring him back to us!"

Some time later the fugitive returned. With tears of genuine repentance he related a strange and touching story. Before his flight he had committed a robbery, but soon had spent his ill-gotten fortune in sinful and extravagant living. Finally he was picked up by the police and arrested as a vagabond. One night, during a violent storm, he succeeded in escaping from the prison, and fled into the interior of a huge forest. He wandered around for hours, but could discover no outlet, and became hopelessly lost. In fear and trembling he fell to the ground and prayed for help and forgiveness. When he raised his eyes—he relates—there before him stood little Jacinta. She took his hand, led him to the edge of the forest, and pointed out the road he should take toward home and safety.

Of course, in the hour of the cousin's deliverance, his visionary guide was sleeping peacefully at home, after spending hours of solicitous prayer in his behalf.

A young man in a neighboring village was imprisoned because of a grave accusation, and if found guilty, would have been sentenced to years of hard labor. His parents asked the shepherds to pray for him to our Lady. On their way to school, Francisco told the other two to proceed to class, but that he would go to church and intercede for the accused.

When they met again, Lucia asked Francisco if he had prayed hard to the Virgin for the grace in question.

"Yes," replied Francisco confidingly, "and you may tell the family that within a few days their son shall come home again—free."

At the time foretold, the prophecy was fulfilled to the letter.

With these three unlettered mountain children, who had seen and conversed with the Queen of Heaven, whose prayers and company were welcomed by thousands who considered them all-powerful intermediaries with the Mother of God—how was it possible that they never, for a moment, entertained a thought of vainglory?

No, thanks be to God and His Blessed Mother, they never succumbed to that! The more they were sought and praised and admired, the more they withdrew from the esteem of the crowds.

In a note of absolute sincerity Lucia has revealed to us in her writings their true convictions and state of mind: "We were annoyed by such servile flattery. As for myself, I felt that everything they said was untrue." And again: "I thank God that then and there, back in the mountains, I knew no such thing as human respect or self-love; that I could stand before anybody with the same simplicity that possessed me in the presence of my parents."

Francisco and Jacinta were equally so disposed. Every word and action was colored and enhanced by the light of joyful, childish moods. A superficial eye might easily fail to discover the slightest difference in any of them.

Mrs. Marto, long after the deaths of her famous children, was asked if she had noticed any great change in their lives after the apparitions.

"Nothing really extraordinary," she replied. "They were always good children." But a profound change had been worked in their souls—in fact, they behaved like saints.

Nothing extraordinary! Nothing but the endless acts of virtue: prayer, sacrifices, and severe self-mortification, in a word, everything that could have excited their interest if the children had not guarded and concealed their sufferings. Only among themselves there were no secrets. In company of others they were silent and backward; but left to themselves, they immediately reverted to their natural tendencies of mutual love and liveliness, never tiring of helping one another in their holy endeavors.

Their mothers often questioned them good-naturedly, but whenever they could conceal their intimate sufferings, they answered only with a smile. One mother would say to the other: "I don't know what has come over the children! They act so mysteriously! We even put our ears to the door when they are alone, but sometimes we can't understand a word they are saying. When someone comes in, they drop their heads, and you can't get a word out of them. It's a puzzle!"

But Jacinta had said to Lucia: "I don't want anybody to know of my sacrifices—nobody but Jesus and Mary!"

And what their "sacrifices" were, we have shown in previous chapters. At the time they were performed, they were known and appreciated by those two great Loves only, and revealed to us later by Lucia, by a specific demand of the ecclesiastical authorities.

Listen to the humility of her cry, in being forced to break her long silence in the cloister: "Until now, it has been possible for me to keep hidden in my soul most of the intimate secrets connected with the apparitions in the Cova da Iria. Today, however, when I am obliged to speak of them, I seek to touch upon them as lightly as possible, so as not to reveal what I hold most sacred. But now that I am bound by obedience—here are the facts...."

Then, as if crushed by this violation of her holiest memories, she continues: "And I remain, alone." (Francisco and Jacinta were long since dead.) "I remain, like a skeleton, stripped of everything, even of my very soul; hung up, as it were, in a museum, to the gaze of visitors, as a record of the misery and the futility of the past" (Letter to the Bishop of Leiria, December 8, 1941).

The reticence and shyness assumed by the children in the presence of strangers is aptly explained by the following story, as told by Lucia in her writings: "One time a priest from Torre Nova came to question us, and because my cousins ran away from him, refusing to answer his questions, I alone was forced to suffer the annoyance. His interrogation was so minute, and so full of quibbling that I began to get scruples as to the accuracy of my answers, feeling that I had told some half-truths. When he had left, I consulted my cousins about the case. It seemed to me that there was no wrong in not telling the entire truth, when someone asked if the Virgin had said 'anything else.' I did not know whether that constituted a lie or not.

"Jacinta said, 'I don't know, either. You are the one who forbids us to speak of it.'

" 'Certainly, I don't want it,' I replied, 'because I am afraid they might begin to ask us just what kind of penances we are doing. God forbid that they should! See now, Jacinta, if you had kept your mouth shut, and told nobody, they would never have known we had seen the Lady, and spoken to her, just as nobody knows, even now, that the angel appeared to us! Besides, it wasn't necessary that they should know it.'

"Time went on, then another priest came just like the previous one with the same questions, the same quibbling, the same laughing and game-making. When he left, my doubts were doubled. I didn't know what to do! 'O my God,' I prayed, 'O my little Mother who is in heaven, you know I do not wish to offend you by lying—but you know, too, that it will not do to tell everything you said to me!'

"One morning we were to be interrogated by a priest, who, they said, was capable of reading one's thoughts. He would tell whether we told the truth or not. Jacinta was overjoyed. Clapping her hands she cried: 'If it is true that he can tell what you are thinking, then he must see that we are not hiding anything!' "

The mind-reader did his very best to uncover their faults, but was finally convinced that truth could be related to humility, and that these wise children knew full well how to unite them.

Humility is self-effacement.

One day, a large, rich-looking automobile pulled up about a hundred feet away from them, and from its interior there emerged a group of men and women, elegantly dressed.

"Wait! And see if they come over to us!" said one of the children.

"No! Let's run!" said a second.

"That would only draw their attention! Let's keep on going. They don't know who we are!"

But the strangers halted them. They were caught. They must think up some means of escape.

"Are you from Aljustrel?" began one of the strangers.

"Yes, sir."

"Do you know the three shepherds to whom our Lady appeared?"

"O yes, we know them very well!"

"Could you tell us where they live?"

"Surely!" And they pointed out the way to their homes.

The strangers left, thanking the children profusely for the information.

The children considered it a great joke, and Jacinta remarked: "See, we should do that every time!"

PART SIX

The Lady Returns

Francisco

Lucia tells the following story: "We were watching the sheep one day in a pasture belonging to my uncles. The far end of it which was cultivated bordered on another property. I said to the cousins: 'You two stay here, while I go and drive the flock away from the crops.'

" 'No, No,' cried Jacinta, 'send Francisco to do it! I want to be with you!'

"Francisco agreed, saying: 'I, too, would rather stay here, but I will go and I shall offer this sacrifice for all sinners!'

"He left, going in the direction of a little thicket of pine trees that divided the two properties. Some time later I said to Jacinta: 'Poor Francisco! All by himself up there! Go, Jacinta, and keep him company for awhile!'

"She consented this time, and away she went. She went into the thicket, but he was not there. She called his name again and again. No answer. Frightened, she came running back to me, sobbing bitterly, thinking the brother was lost.

" 'I'll find him,' I said consolingly. 'Wait here for me!'

"I searched and called his name. No sight of him, and still no answer. I looked everywhere. Finally I found him. Behind a low wall of stones, he was on his knees, his head bent to the ground. I approached him, touched his shoulder—then called him by name loudly. Raising his head, he looked bewildered, like one coming out of deep slumber.

" 'Were you praying, Francisco?'

" 'Yes—I began to say the prayer of the Angel …then I became lost in thought!'

" 'Didn't you hear Jacinta calling you?'

" 'I heard nothing!'

"I told him to go back to his sister who was crying for him. He turned to go,…then quickly changed his mind and came back again at once, saying he wished to be alone, to offer this sacrifice to God for sinners. He went to the spot where I had found him, and where he had lost himself in meditation. His soul, thirsting for things supernatural, was moved with an insatiable desire to prolong this union with God."

Francisco was a quiet, gentle, silent boy—but courageous. Prominent among his best characteristics was an extreme delicacy of conscience and a ready willingness to submit to others. With a spirit less expansive than Jacinta's, he rarely expressed any desires of his own, preferring always to do the bidding of Lucia and his little sister.

With the soul of a poet, he loved and admired all nature, being especially fond of birds. He imitated their songs, trained them to come and share his food, guarded their nests and could not suffer to see anybody do them the slightest harm.

Once he met a boy carrying a goldfinch in his hand, and, full of pity for the little captive, he gave the boy four small pieces of money, his whole fortune, in exchange for the prisoner. Then joyfully he threw the goldfinch into the air, crying: "Now watch yourself, and don't be caught again!"

In this way he revealed that tenderness of spirit that moved him always to have compassion for the sufferings of others, even if dumb animals.

From the days of the Apparition, when he was wrapped in ecstatic levitation at least three times, the beautiful Lady had conferred upon him the gift of heavenly contemplation. His days were spent in close communion with God and the Blessed Virgin, praying and meditating on the messages he had received from them, but he was dominated principally by the offenses to almighty God.

"Francisco, what gives you the most satisfaction: to console the dear Lord, or to pray for the conversion of sinners, that they may escape eternal punishment?" Lucia once asked him.

He answered: "I would much rather console the dear Lord. Didn't you notice how sad our Lady was when she said we were not to offend our Lord, who was already so much grieved! First I would console Him, then pray for sinners that they might sin no more."

Since the apparitions, Francisco had developed a tendency to detach himself from his companions, to steal away into the rocks and trees, there to pray and meditate. His prayers at such times consisted not so much of lengthy verbal ones, but more of recollection and contemplation, wholly immersed in things divine.

In his conversation with Lucia and his sister he would sometimes reveal his interior life: "The Angel was beautiful; and the Virgin was far more beautiful—but what gave me my greatest joy was to see the Lord in that dazzling light. Oh, how it pleased me to see Him."

When Jacinta would say that the "lights" of the beautiful Lady were prettier because they did not burn or blind, he would say, almost pityingly:

"Oh, no, Jacinta, no light is like that which comes from our Lord!"

"We stood," he would say, "in that fiercely burning light which is God Himself and we were not consumed. What are You, O Lord? We shall never be able to understand it. But what a shame that He should be so sad! If I only were able to console Him!"

One day, Lucia's mother invited the three shepherds into the house to have some honey-water. She first offered the glass to Francisco, but the little gentleman passed it on to the youngest, Jacinta. While she sipped the beverage, Francisco stole away, unobserved, from the party. Going into the garden a short few minutes later, the two girls found him by the spring and asked him why he had not taken the honey-water, and why he had made no answer when his mother called him several times to come in and join them. He answered: "When I took the glass in my hand, the thought occurred to me that I could offer that sweet drink as a sacrifice of consolation to the Lord, and then I ran out here."

On another occasion, Lucia and Jacinta were amusing themselves by capturing butterflies. They would first hold the beautiful creatures in their hands for a few moments, intrigued and delighted with the riotous colors and designs on their wings, and then they would release them, offering their possession as a sacrifice of self-denial. When lunch time came, they began to look around for Francisco, who as soon as they had arrived at the pasture, had gone to a high ledge of rock, there to pray and meditate, unobserved and uninterrupted. When

Lucia and Jacinta found him, they called to him to come and eat with them. He answered, saying he did not wish to eat just then.

"But you will pray the rosary with us after lunch, will you not?"

"Oh, yes," he replied. "I will do that. Call me when you are ready."

When questioned later about his long and solitary meditation upon the rocky ledge, he informed them: "I spent the whole time thinking of the dear Lord, so saddened by the sins of the world. I wish I could console Him."

What a noble ideal—to console God who has been offended by the sins of the world!

A Light by the Door

Frequently when Lucia and Jacinta wished to converse or amuse themselves, they would see Francisco about to retire to some solitary spot to pray. Although they would try to detain him, he would hold aloft his beloved beads smilingly and significantly and say: "Don't you remember what the Lady said: that I must pray many, many rosaries before I enter heaven!"

"But we can pray the rosary later on!"

"When you do, I will join you."

Indeed, his days on earth were short, and judging from the feverish acceleration of his piety and perfection, he must have been warned of the impending termination.

In the last few months of World War I, the end of which was predicted by our Lady, there came over Europe an epidemic that destroyed more lives than had the terrible war itself. They called it the Spanish Plague. It was similar to, if not the same as, the devastating scourge called the "influenza" that ravaged the Americas in 1918. Its toll could be counted in the twenty millions.

Portugal was no exception, and finally, the dread disease struck Fatima and its surroundings. The entire Marto family fell to it, except the father. On December 23, 1918, Francisco became very ill. After fifteen days he was able to leave his bed, but the fever had sapped his strength. He had no desire for food, so that gradually his weakened body succumbed to the deathly sickness.

If the day was warm and bright he would slowly wend his way to the church in Fatima to spend as much time as his strength would allow before his Eucharistic Jesus. Sometimes, when his longing became irresistible, he dragged himself painfully up the rocky mount to the Cova to the blessed spot where he had seen the Lady "clothed as the sun"; where his soul had been suffused with divine grace and light. He would kneel before the little oak in a delirium of joy, his eyes fixed as though he were again enjoying the vision of his heavenly Queen. He prayed: "Oh, how I desire to come and stay with you, my sweet Lady!"

He would seem entirely renewed when he returned from such excursions, and his happiness found its reflection in his enlivened cheeks and eyes. The neighbors would tell him how much better he was looking, that he would soon be well again. Little did they know of the heavenly nostalgia that filled his heart night and day.

Toward the end of February, 1919, his condition became worse. Jacinta, the little angel, hardly ever left his bedside, helping him in all his needs. His beloved ones prayed unceasingly for his recovery, and suggested the offering of a solemn novena to their beloved Lady of Fatima, who had thus far so signally honored them, and helped others in their hour of need.

"It is of no use!" the boy would murmur. "Your prayers shall not be answered!"

In his very presence, his godmother made a vow to the Virgin of Fatima, that if he should recover, she would donate a quantity of grain equal to his own weight. Francisco only shook his head, saying there would be no recovery. Headstrong obstinacy was the interpretation of his dear ones for this attitude of his, not knowing what secrets he guarded in his heart. How were they to know that the beautiful Lady had appeared to him again in his sickness to tell him that she would soon come and take him into heaven!

How joyfully he counted the hours, the few short hours that still separated him from eternal bliss and happiness with his beloved Lord and Queen. He was now too weak to say more than a decade or two of the rosary, or to repeat as often as he wished the offertory prayers that Mary and the Angel had taught him, but he had told his mother to lead with the verbal invocations and he would follow her with mental responses.

In his illness we also have the opportunity of hearing the last, inexpressible echoes of the ideal aspiration that governed all his thoughts and actions towards the end of his life—the consolation of his God.

No sooner had Lucia and Jacinta entered his room one morning when he warned them: "You mustn't talk too much today, because my head hurts so much!"

Taking no offense Jacinta promptly suggested: "Don't forget to offer up your headache for sinners!"

"Oh, yes!" he replied, "but first of all, I offer it up to console our Lord and the Virgin—then for the sinners—and then for the Holy Father.

"I wonder if the good Lord will still be so sad?" he asked, preoccupied in his thoughts. "It makes me feel bad to see Him like that!

"I will offer to Him every sacrifice that I am able to make," he assured Lucia, who tells us that in all his sufferings he never uttered one sigh of lament.

She asked him on another occasion: "Francisco, do you suffer much?"

"Yes," he answered, "but I bear it all for the sake of our Lord and the Virgin." Later on, he entrusted to Lucia the knotted cord that he had worn about his waist. "Take it away," he said, "before Mamma sees it. I am not able to carry it any longer!"

"He accepted every little service his mother did for his comfort," Lucia continues to tell, "but I could never detect on any occasion that he was pleased or displeased by these."

Then the day of his departure into heaven approached.

On April 2nd, two days before the end, the symptoms of death set in. His one regret was communicated to his mother: "Mamma, must I die without receiving Jesus in the Blessed Sacrament?"

The mother comforted him, promising to send for the pastor, who would hear his confession, and perhaps give him permission to make his First Holy Communion.

Confession?—What a problem for an innocent child of God, and privileged child of Mary! He called for Lucia, to come immediately. "Lucia," he whispered, as she leaned over his pillow—"today I must make my confession in order to receive my First Holy Communion—before I die! Do you know of any sins I may have committed?"

She hesitated—"Well...you disobeyed your mamma several times when she told you to stay at home, and instead you came with us, or hid yourself away somewhere to pray. Remember?"

"Yes, I did, that is true!" he replied, and lowered his head in sorrow.... "Go now to Jacinta and ask her if she remembers anything that I should confess." The little sister recalled that before the apparitions, he had stolen a few cents from his father to buy a harmonica, and that he was one of the boys from Aljustrel, who, in make-believe war, had hurled stones at the boys from Beleiros.

"I have already confessed those sins," he said, "but I will confess them again. Maybe those sins have made the Lord sad. Even if I did not have to die, I would never sin like that again. I am very sorry for them!"

Folding his hands he prayed: "O my Jesus, pardon these sins!" He turned again to Lucia, saying: "Lucia, you too pray to the Lord for pardon for me!"

"I will, but you can be sure they are pardoned, Francisco, from the time the Lady said she would come and take you into heaven. I am on my way to Mass now, and I shall pray to Jesus in the tabernacle for you."

His face lit up with gratitude for Lucia's consoling words.

When the priest came and heard his confession, and consented that he should receive the Blessed Sacrament on the following day, a great joy filled his heart and he kept repeating over and over—"Tomorrow! Tomorrow! I shall receive

Jesus!" He told his mother to give him nothing to drink after midnight, as he wished to observe a strict fast before Holy Communion.

Early next morning, when the priest came into his room carrying the Sacred Host, he requested that he be allowed to sit up on the edge of the bed and confess his sins once more; for he desired his soul to be as pure as an angel before receiving his beloved Lord.

After Holy Communion, his soul was flooded with happiness. The same Lord, whom he had so perseveringly striven to console, was now in his very heart, consoling him.

"Today I am happier than you are, Jacinta," he said teasingly to his little sister, who was permitted to be present at the coming of the Eucharistic Lord into their home and who was watching and admiring the religious fervor of the dying boy.

He hoped he would not die until he could receive Jesus again. But that was not to be. His First Holy Communion was also his Viaticum.

During the day his condition became worse, but he did not complain of any pain. Toward evening, after reciting the rosary with Lucia and Jacinta, as well as he could in his extreme weakness he bade them farewell. "I am going to heaven," he told them, "and there I shall ask the Lady to reunite us before long.... Goodbye, till we meet again—in heaven!"

"In heaven!" they answered. "And be sure," added Lucia, "to pray for sinners, and for the Holy Father, and for Jacinta and me!"

"I will," he said, "but you better tell Jacinta to do all that, because I am afraid I'll forget when I look at the good Lord. I am going to spend all my time consoling Him!"

The sorrowing godmother now came into the room and approached his bed. The humble child asked her to bless him and to pardon him for any trouble he might ever have caused her. And as night descended, his last night on earth, he begged pardon and benediction from all who were present.

About six o'clock the next morning they heard a cry: "Mamma! Mamma!"

She had never left the bedside of the dying child, weeping and mourning for him, who was doubly dear to her now. "What is it, my love! What is it you wish?" she asked, stifling her grief.

"See! Mamma!... There!... By the door! Oh, what a beautiful light!"—It was the same celestial light that he had seen six times in the apparitions.

To please him the mother looked towards the door, but seeing nothing, thought the boy was in a delirium.

"Beautiful Light," he kept murmuring, fascinated and enlivened by the Vision. He tried to rise, his hands extended before him—to approach the Light. A prolonged smile illuminated his features— the smile of paradise, that death itself dare not obliterate.

The Lady had come for him, just as she had promised, in the brightness of eternal glory.

Francisco Marto had left the earth without a struggle or agony, in the attitude of one departing to a better life, and accompanied by a beloved friend. It was on Friday, April 4, 1919; he had not yet reached his eleventh year.

This youth had died as he had lived—in a humility and obscurity that befitted his vocation and formed his character, with his eyes on the Light that had guided and instructed him in his earthly days. Seemingly of secondary importance during the days of the apparitions, he remained a most mystifying figure, withdrawing himself as much as possible from worldly companionship and devoting all his time to the contemplation of the heavenly revelations of the visions. Like a modest little violet, off from the beaten path, a "flower born to blush unseen," he shrank from the eyes of a curious world, and the fragrance of his purity and innocence shall not be wasted on a sinful world.

Of his earthly remains there exists today only a small quantity of dust and bones, which have been interred alongside the uncorrupted body of his saintly sister Jacinta. The first lamp of the Sanctuary of Fatima was herewith extinguished from our gaze, only to be rekindled in a brighter blaze of glory and inspiration before the throne of the Most High, and at the feet of the Queen of Peace—a perpetual consolation of the dear Lord, whom he strove so valiantly on earth to appease for the sins of his ungrateful brethren.

For this was the mission of Francisco, the little shepherd!

Jacinta's Sufferings

The prolonged suffering and bereavement of her little brother was a heavy blow to the sensitive and affectionate Jacinta. With a heavy heart, but sustained by the sweet memories of the events of the past, she now rarely left her home.

Finding her so pensive and sad, they would ask her: "Jacinta, what are you thinking about?"

"About Francisco," she would reply. "Oh, if I could only see him once more!"

She was depressed, as a child might be, but still mindful of her obligations. Shortly before he died, Jacinta had given Francisco a most ingenious little message that he was to take to heaven for her: "Tell Jesus and the Lady that I greet them with all my love. And tell them that I will suffer everything for the good of sinners, and for reparation to the Immaculate Heart of Mary."

How thoroughly this child had learned and taken to heart the lesson of self-immolation imparted in the visions of the Sorrowful Mother. Only such souls know that divine love must be repaid with love, and that love is tempered most by a full measure of sufferings, endured for the sake of the Lover, who thirsts for the salvation of everyone.

Heaven received Jacinta's heroic offer. It was accepted and ratified. The sentence: a consuming illness, to burden the rest of her days.

She already knew that she would soon be taken by the Virgin to rejoin Francisco in heaven, but she knew neither the day nor the year. In the meantime, in accordance with the wish of the Beautiful Lady, when asked if she was ready to suffer anything and everything for the salvation of sinners, she had replied with a willing and a gracious "Yes!" Thereupon the Virgin revealed to her that she would be taken to two hospitals, to suffer vicariously for sinners, to make reparation for the offenses against the Immaculate Heart and the Heart of Jesus, and finally, that life itself would be demanded of her, far from home and her loved ones.

The first part of the prophecy was now about to be fulfilled, and the remainder was to unfold itself thereafter in a quick succession of events.

After six months of a siege of the influenza, the malady progressed into a state of purulent pleurisy. She was taken to St. Augustine's Hospital in Villanova de Ourem, where she was confined for two months, July and August of 1919. No sign of recovery being noticed, she was returned to her home in Aljustrel.

Her sufferings were many. The very sight of food was repugnant to her, especially milk. One morning her mother tried to get her to take a cup. "Mother, I don't want it!" she cried, as she turned her head away and smothered her nausea. The mother insisted gently, but, when again repulsed, demurred: "I really don't know what to give you. Everything disagrees with you so!"

Lucia, who had no fear of the epidemic, was a faithful nurse to the stricken child in these days of almost universal death and suffering. She was present when the incident mentioned above took place. "Is it possible, Jacinta," she intervened, "that you would disobey your mother! Are you going to lose this opportunity of making a great sacrifice for our Lord?"

Tearfully Jacinta replied that she had not thought of that, and summoning her mother she expressed her sorrow and repentance for her rudeness, and a readiness, in the future, to accept anything her mother might offer her. She drank the milk when brought to her again without a sign of repugnance, but confided to Lucia later on: "If you only knew what it cost me to take it!"

She confessed later that she found it increasingly disagreeable to partake of broth or milk, but that she gulped it down with a prayer of sacrifice out of love for Jesus and His sweet Mother.

Once the mother thought to please her by adding a bunch of grapes to the dreaded diet of milk. She had always been fond of grapes. "Take the grapes away, Mother! I'll drink the milk!" And she drank the sickening milk as though it were the tastiest and most preferred drink she had ever been offered. The nausea was conquered. A good sign, thought the anxious mother, as she left the room. She did not know that Jacinta, just then, was whispering into the ear of the smiling Lucia: "I so wished to have the grapes instead, but I offered that up as another sacrifice!"

Every morning it was necessary to medicate a large, festering sore on her breast, which caused her excruciating pain. Someone perhaps had unknowingly neglected the strict rule of hygienic treatment, so that infections set in, increasing her torment considerably. But she never uttered a word of complaint. When Lucia would ask her if she suffered much, she would reply: "Yes, I suffer very much; but all for the conversion of sinners, and for the offenses against the Immaculate Heart of the Virgin."

Coming into the room on another occasion, Lucia found her very exhausted looking.

"Do you feel worse today than usual?" she asked.

"I suffered much last night, but as a sacrifice for the dear Lord I denied myself the comfort of changing my position in bed. After that I did not sleep at all."

When the pain of her malady became most acute, she would lament with a truly Christian heroism: "My head aches, and I am very thirsty, but I will take nothing to drink, for the sake of Jesus and poor sinners!"

She asked Lucia one day: "How many sacrifices did you make last night for our Lord?"

"I got up three times to say the prayer of the angel," Lucia replied.

Jacinta said: "I made lots and lots of them! I couldn't count them! With every pain, I refused to cry or complain!"

She was very candid with Lucia, as was to be expected, as no secrets could possibly exist between those who had shared the love and the favors of Mary. To Lucia she confessed the severity and the extent of her suffering, but begged her to withhold the information from her mother, for whose consolation she always tried to appear cheerful and free from pain. Her friends and relations, too, when they called and asked her if they could fetch something she liked, were misled by her innocent deception: "No, thank you. I don't need anything. I am feeling fine!"

Beyond Lucia, she desired that no one should pierce the veil of her sacrificial torments except the dear Lord and the beautiful Lady.

The best testimonial we have of the heroism of this young and penetrating soul, who constantly presented a sublime sense of dutiful fulfillment of her vocation, is contained in the following words of Lucia: "The second time I visited her in the hospital of St. Augustine in Villanova, I found her as cheerful as ever, and equally prompt to suffer for God, for the Immaculate Heart of Mary, for the Holy Father and for the salvation of sinners. She thought of nothing else. It was her ideal, and the one subject of her conversation. It dominated all her thoughts—like a divine obsession."

To her physical agonies, there was added another torment, that began with her illness, and increased in intensity every hour. It was the daily visits of inconsiderate strangers, the unfailing curious crowds, who came and sat by her bedside, staring or asking questions. Some, of course, came with the proper spirit of edification, and conducted themselves accordingly. Interpreting the thoughts of this latter group, let us listen to Lucia, who was well familiar with this phase of popular psychology, from the days of the apparitions up to the particular moment we refer to.

"For myself," she affirms, "I felt myself in the presence of a sanctity that was closely allied to God. Her attitude was grave and modest, but pleasing. Her thoughts and speech were those of an adult, and her virtue advanced far beyond her tender age. In every action there was revealed in her the presence of the Divinity."

When she was well, she hid, or astutely withdrew from the gaze of the public. However, helpless in her infirmity, she could only bear it in silence, or, as Lucia assures us, turn it into another meritorious work of mercy, in reparation for sinners.

Jacinta's Plea Refused

Young as she was, the soul of Jacinta was rich in the memories of many hallowed spots in and around her native village, and, as she advanced toward her crown of martyrdom, it caused her many pangs of sorrow to think that she must soon bid them all good-bye.

One day, Lucia brought her some flowers that she had gathered on the mount of Cabeco, where the children had received the visit of the angel. The memory of those happy days welled up in her eyes as she took the beloved flowers from her cousin. "I shall never return to pray there again," she cried, "nor to Valinhos, nor to the Cova da Iria."

"But Jacinta, that is not so important, considering that you are soon to see the Lord and our Lady!" Lucia consoled her.

"Yes, that's true I should be satisfied." But it was not easy to forget the good times, the sacred experiences, prayers and the celestial visitation of such places as the garden, the grotto of the Cabeco, the Cova and the many solitary pasture lands where no one ever disturbed them in their devotions.

"Lucia, I will never see them again. But you will—without me!—without Francisco!" and great big tears rolled down her cheeks as Lucia, like a little mother, wiped them away, even as her own fell just as bitterly. "You will pray hard for me, won't you, Lucia?"

Though physically far removed from the scenes of her supernatural experiences, where she had learned the prayers that she now loved to repeat so often, the saintly invalid still continued to perform her devotions in a spirit and attitude befitting their celestial origin, as she had always done in the days of robust health. Even exaggeratedly so. When unobserved, she would leave her bed, and prostrate herself on the floor, praying in the prescribed words of the Angel and the Lady.

"Sometimes," she confided to Lucia, "I can't bend my body to the ground, or I would fall over. So I just stay on my knees." It was, of course, an exaggerated penance, considering her frail condition, and the Dean of Ourem, to whom the spiritual direction of Lucia was entrusted, sent word that Jacinta should abstain from leaving her bed for this purpose, and advised that she was to pray in bed so as to conserve her wasting strength.

"Will Jesus be content with that?" Jacinta inquired.

"Surely! It is Jesus' wish that we do everything the Dean tell us to do," Lucia assured her.

"All right, then. I will not get up to pray anymore!"

It had been her delight to go and pray to Jesus, the Prisoner of the Tabernacle. Even her sickness would not have kept her away from Him, but she was persuaded to convey her little messages of love and adoration through the medium of her devoted cousin. "Tell Him I love Him so much, and give Him all my affections!" she would joyfully confide to Lucia. "It does me so much good to repeat over and over that I love the dear Lord, and my heart seems on fire...but it is a fire that does not burn! I hope the dear Lord and the Lady will never let me tire of saying that I love them!"

One of her dearest possessions was the rope that she had constantly worn about her waist, next to her body, in a spirit of self-mortification. It had three large knots in it, and it was stained with blood, exactly as was the one that Francisco had worn.

Sensing the approach of death, she gave the instrument of torture to Lucia.

"Take care of it," she said, "and be sure that Mamma does not see it, for if I should happen to be cured I will want to have it again." Thus did she regretfully separate herself from the different modes and means of torture that she had gladly assumed in obedience to heaven's instructions that she offer constant prayer and sacrifice in reparation for the sins of others.

Lucia destroyed the two ropes, one of which had been worn by Francisco, depriving the world of precious relics connected with the historical wonders of Fatima.

The increasing weakness caused by her sickness was gradually forcing Jacinta to lighten the burden of her immolations, but she knew that one of the greatest sacrifices she had ever made was soon to be encountered, and it alone was more bitter than all the others combined: separation from Lucia—her cousin, confidant, teacher and ideal.

Their two hearts beat as one, their souls were in perfect accord. Together they had looked upon the ineffable beauty of the Queen of Heaven, had listened in rapture to the sweet melody of her accents in prayer and heavenly instruction, so that now their souls were cemented in a union little short of that of the eternally blessed. What was physical suffering compared to the joy of having Lucia by her side, to console her and remind her of the imminent joys of heaven? What a happiness to pour out her heart to this second mother of hers, who knew all the secrets of her soul, and who understood every thought and action and sacrifice as a manifestation of the fruits of the apparitions! No matter how severe, how foolish, how extravagant her self-mortification appeared to others, Lucia understood—and Lucia alone understood!

For the first time the tortured little victim must have cried to the beautiful Lady for help, for the Lady came to her—came personally—but only to ask a final, crushing sacrifice.

The last and only human consolation she desired was denied her. Desolate and sorrowful she revealed to Lucia: "I asked the Lady to let you come with me to the other hospital—and she refused. None of my sufferings was like this one. She said Mamma would take me there, and then I was to stay there all alone! Oh, if you only could come alone with me! To be separated from you shall be the greatest sorrow of my life!" Humbly she lowered her head in resignation, but bitter, precious tears rolled down her pallid cheeks. When finally she had checked her emotion, a new light and strength lit up her eyes, and she exclaimed: "But let it be so! This, too, I will offer up for the love of Jesus; for reparation to the pure heart of Mary; for sinners and for the Holy Father!"

One morning as Lucia went into the sick room unexpectedly, she saw the child kissing and caressing a picture of our Lady: "O dear little Mother of heaven, so I must die all alone!" The Virgin had come again, in response to her childish insistence, but only to predict more trials, and to instruct her regarding past predictions.

Noticing Lucia's approach the invalid turned and said: "The Lady has told me that I must go to Lisbon, to another hospital—that I shall never see you nor my parents again—that there are more sufferings to come—and that I shall die alone. But I was to be brave, for she would come soon and take me into heaven."

"And when you go to heaven," Lucia interrupted, to distract her thoughts of dying alone, "what will you do?"

Her features brightened and the pale lips parted in a smile of anticipation: "In heaven—I will love Jesus and Mary so much! I will ask them to help you, and the Holy Father, and my parents and brothers and sisters, and all who have asked me to pray for them, and all sinners!"

In the strange ways of divine Providence, there came a sudden fulfillment of the prophetic words of the Virgin, as revealed by the invalid. Toward the end of January, 1920, there came to Fatima in a pilgrimage the celebrated specialist Dr. Henry Lisboa, who sought the acquaintance of the surviving children. Finding the younger one in such a pitiful condition, he begged permission to take her to the metropolis, in hopes of saving her life with a surgical operation.

The entire Marto family was opposed to the suggestions, at first, but finally, like all good mothers, fearful of the loss of her child, Mrs. Marto consented.

"It was the last time I was to see her alive," Lucia writes, in describing the departure, "and she was still grieving that she must die far from her loved ones.

" 'Do not think of us!' I told her.

" 'No, no! the more I think, the more I suffer for sinners. After all, our Lady will come for me!'

"Sobbing, she embraced me, holding me to herself for a long time," continues Lucia's account of the parting. " 'I shall never, never see you again! You can't be with me, but pray for me, very much, until I go to heaven. Up there I will remember you. Don't tell anybody the secret, even if they kill you for it. Love Jesus and the Immaculate Heart of Mary with all your heart, and make many sacrifices for sinners!' "

It was, indeed, the final farewell. They were never to meet again on earth. Poor Jacinta! The separations from friends, family, relations, and most of all from Lucia, nearly broke her heart. Under any circumstances, it was a terrifying ordeal for a child of nine years to be torn from the bosom of the family and sent into a distant city among strangers without love or sympathy. Of course, Jacinta did not realize it at the time, but these separations were a part of God's designs for her, that she might be lifted to a higher sphere of sanctity, totally lost to herself and the world.

She was to be matured for heaven.

The Flickering Light

Accompanied by her mother, as our Lady had predicted, Jacinta was taken to Lisbon, where they had been offered the hospitality of a certain rich family; but when they saw the pitiful condition she was in, their door was closed to Jacinta. Finally she found refuge in the Orphanage of Our Lady of the Miracles. Here she felt more at home.

The Mother Superior herself, Sister Mary of the Purification (her family name was Godinho), reserved for herself the honor of personally nursing the little child, and she acquitted herself of this task with such loving kindness and charity and maternal delicacy, that the grateful invalid named her *madrina*—"little mother."

And what joy it afforded her to be under the same roof with the hidden Jesus, in the tabernacle of the chapel of the institute. Many happy hours did she spend with Him, in peace and contentment. What a perfect happiness it was to receive Him daily into her heart, in perfect union through day and night!

From the official ecclesiastical inquiry, compiled from records of Sister Mary of the Purification, we extract here a few notes relating to the characteristics of the young patient: "spends no time in self-amusement—takes very little nourishment—never complains of her sickness—recites the rosary daily—truthful and reprehensive towards deceit. For devotion she generally goes to a gallery that faces into the chapel, and chooses a place that affords a clear view of the altar. And when she prays, her attitude and the expression of her features make a most profound impression as she fixes her gaze in rapture upon the tabernacle."

The specialist who had been instrumental in bringing her to Lisbon made all preparations for the operation. The little one objected, insisting that it would be useless, since the Virgin had told her before her departure that she would go to Lisbon, and there she would die.

Nevertheless, she had to submit to it. On the feast of the Purification of the Blessed Virgin she made her confession, received Communion, and later tearfully bade a fond farewell to Jesus in the tabernacle. She left the institute—familiarly named by her "Our Lady of Fatima"—and was taken to the hospital D. Estefania. The operation took place there on February 10, the vigil of the feast of the apparition of Our Lady at Lourdes.

Because of her extreme weakness, a local anesthetic was administered, thus leaving her conscious of every movement.

An opening was made in her side by removing two ribs in the region of the heart.

On the following day began the interminable martyrdom of medication, and I use the word martyrdom advisedly, because her sufferings were indescribably severe. Through it all her only expression was a weak and prayerful: "O my Lady! O Mother of mine!"

After several medications the pains were so excruciating that she confided to her beloved *madrina*: "I'm afraid I can't stand it any longer!"

"Courage, little one!" she would reply, passing her hand gently over the cold-sweated brow of the child. "Courage! Suffer with patience! This pleases our Lord very much!"

At first, the operation seemed to have been successful. A change set in, however; soon her condition was worse than ever.

Meanwhile, several nurses and visitors came to see her. According to the standard of the innocent child, they were dressed in a manner that was shockingly immodest.

"Why do they do such things!" she remarked later. "Have they no idea of what eternity is like? The Virgin told me that it is the sins of the flesh that drags souls into hell—that we must avoid such wanton sins!—that we must do penance and reflect on our evil doings!" And thinking of the grief of the Virgin as she disclosed these facts to her, she added: "How sorry I was for the Lady! How sorry!"

Two competent physicians were now put in charge of her case. She was very gracious toward them and grateful also, for one of the doctors told her that the only recompense he desired for his services was to be remembered in her prayers. Jacinta thanked him and replied that she would gladly be a partner to such a good bargain. Then looking intently into his unsuspicioning eyes, she startled him by saying: "You shall follow me soon into eternity."

A similar prophecy was made to another doctor who came to her recommending himself to her prayers to our Lady. She promised, but added the astounding revelation that he would die shortly after her demise, and not only that, but that his daughter was also to die before him.

The mother of Jacinta came down to Lisbon one day to visit her daughter. In conversation with the Mother Superior of the orphanage, the latter asked Mrs. Marto whether any of her daughters at home had ever expressed a desire to enter the religious life. The good woman, whether from ignorance, or from prejudice against convent life, which may be discovered in the most unusual places, replied: "God forbid!"

Jacinta was scandalized: "I would like to enter a convent," she said bravely, "but I like still more the thought of soon entering heaven!" And when the opportunity presented itself, she whispered to Mother Superior: "The Virgin would be pleased to have my sisters give their lives to God as nuns, but Mamma will not allow it. For this the Virgin is coming soon to take them away from her into heaven!

"And you, *Madrina*," added the little prophetess, knowing how much the sister longed to go to the consecrated scene of the apparitions someday, "shall go to Fatima...but only after my death!"

Every one of these predictions were fulfilled.

Regarding the last one, by force of a most unusual concession on the part of her superiors, the *madrina* was permitted to accompany Jacinta's funeral cortege back to Villanova, and from there it was but a short journey farther to the hallowed shrine of the Cova da Iria.

The last days of the little angel were filled with physical agonies. She enjoyed the privilege of many more communications from her beloved Lady.

The kind sister came every day to visit her in the hospital, and her presence dispelled for the invalid that air of austerity and strange distinction that pervades such institutions, so that it was not difficult for Jacinta to open her heart to her foster-mother, the *madrina*, who was so solicitous for her welfare.

Often, as the sister passed or sat by her bed, the child would exclaim: "Please stand to one side, *Madrina*. That is where the Lady stood when she was here."

The sister was thoroughly frightened one morning, when entering the room she heard the patient exclaim: "Come later, *Madrina!* I am expecting the Lady now!"—and a luminous cloud came and hovered above the bed. With her eyes fixed on the celestial presence, the child went into an ecstasy of happiness.

What new tidings did our Lady have for her privileged daughter? And is it any wonder that wisdom and prophecy fell so readily from the blessed lips of this unlettered shepherdess from the mountains of Aljustrel! Listen to the depth and grandeur of some of her sayings as recorded by the beloved *madrina*, her nurse!

"Our Lady told me that the sins that cause the loss of most souls are the sins of impurity. There shall appear certain styles of clothing that shall be offensive to our Lord. People who wish to serve God have no need of style. The Church has no styles, because the Lord is always the same."

"The world must abandon its impurity, and not remain obstinately in iniquity, as it is now."

"The Virgin said that the world would be tortured by discord and many wars. Wars are nothing else but castigations for sin."

"The Blessed Mother can no longer support the arm of her beloved Son extended over the world."

"We must do much penance. If we repent, the Lord will pardon the world; if not, punishment shall come upon it."

"Self-mortification and sacrifice are very pleasing to Jesus."

"If men knew the meaning of eternity, they would do anything to mend their lives."

"If the government would permit the Church in peace and freedom to exercise the Catholic faith, it would be blessed by God."

"Priests should occupy themselves solely with the things of the Church and of the soul. They should be most pure of heart."

"The rebellion of priests and religious against their proper superiors and the Holy Father is most displeasing to God."

"Dear *Madrina*, pray incessantly for priests, religious, sinners and the heads of government."

"Dear *Madrina*, avoid every luxury; desire no riches; love poverty and silence. Be very charitable, even to those who seek to harm you. Speak ill of no one, and avoid the company of those who talk about their neighbors."

"Be very patient! Patience leads the way to heaven."

"To be a religious it is necessary to be very pure in body and soul."

The sister asked her once: "Do you know what that means—to be pure?"

"Yes, I know! I know what it means! To be pure of body means to keep the law of chastity; to be pure of mind means to commit no offenses, not to look at forbidden things, not to lie but always to tell the truth, no matter what it costs."

"But who has taught you these things?" the sister asked, in pardonable wonder.

"Our Lady!"

These wise words of instruction and warning and prophecy from the nine-year-old child were the last earthly fickerings of a light that was presently to shine forth like a star of the first magnitude in the firmament of heaven.

Knowing that her time was short, she intensified with the declining hours the zeal for good that consumed her innocent soul. She would use up the last spark of life, praying, counseling, admonishing and reproving, to enkindle the sacred flame of love, and tranquilly to diffuse her own dying light: like a little lamp on the altar of sacrifice, whose oil running low, throws a bright flame just before it goes out.

Fragrance of the "Little Angel"

Four days before Jacinta's death, just when the load of suffering became too heavy to bear and she was tempted to cry, "Enough, O Lord!"—the spasms of pain were quieted, her cry of anguish was hushed, and a great peace came over her.

She could hardly wait for Sister Mary to come, to tell her the wonderful news: "Just think of it, *Madrina!* I have nothing to complain about any longer. Our Lady came again"—(how natural she made this seem!)—"and told me soon she will take me away with her, and since then all my pains have disappeared!"

This was a prelude and an announcement that soon she would come into the fatherland where no pain exists, and where joy is everlasting.

From Lisbon she also had it made known to Lucia that the Virgin had told the day and the very hour of her death.

She asked for the sacraments. On Friday evening, February 20, 1920, she made her confession, and begged for the Viaticum. Thinking she would live many hours yet, her wish was not granted.

That same night, at 10:30, the Queen of the Rosary, her Beautiful Lady, came and led her into eternal peace and happiness.

The fortunate children of Fatima were faithful, even heroically faithful, to the noble mission of reparation and expiation of universal sin, especially of sensuality and lust. Because they were clean of heart, they knew of the sins of the flesh only through the revelations of the vision. Once the eternal devastation of such sins were pointed out to them, their pure hearts and loving souls could never cease to wish by every means to appease the wrath of an outraged Divinity.

How true it is that converted sinners and the saints of all time have been souls animated by a great desire for penitence, repressing their own evil instincts and atoning for the sins of a forgetful and ungrateful world. But in this case, it was a question of three innocent children who had never heard the roar of the beast in their souls. Chaste in body and mind, they penetrated to a supernatural enlightenment that raised them to a celestial likeness of the angel who initiated them into the novitiate of atonement that was to be refined and perfected in the subsequent ministry of the Virgin. Like the Child of Nazareth, under her motherly care, they "grew in wisdom and grace before God and man." Their hearts conformed to hers.

Sin is like an ulcerous sore on a body otherwise fair and beautiful. It is a disorder. It is a monstrosity. What then must be the abhorrence against this unruly enthronement of self-love opposite the throne of the King of kings, the Author of all good, when the veil of nature is drawn back revealing the utter devastation and desolation of hell, the creation of sin, which the innocent children were privileged to see by the grace and favor of the Immaculate Mother of God.

They had signified a willingness to plead for rebellious souls, to participate more directly in the work of God's Redemption, to help carry the cross of Calvary.

Suffering is the way of living the mystery of the Redemption. If Christ, the Son of God, saw fit to shed His last drop of blood to expiate our sins and to curb our rebellious instincts, then suffering properly assumed is nothing else on earth but the shadow of His real presence in our lives.

Therefore, we should not be scandalized by the apparent "cruelties" of the apparition of Fatima: the burdensome secrets, the self-punishment and sacrifices, the persecutions, the painful illness and premature deaths that we witness in the careers of the shepherds of Aljustrel.

We have their prototype in St. Bernadette Soubirous, the seer of the apparitions in the grotto of Massabielle. The Virgin told her: "I do not promise you happiness in this world, but only in the next." Trials and tribulations, sickness, physical and spiritual afflictions, misunderstandings and ridicule—that was her altar of self-immolation, from the first visitation of the Immaculate Conception to the end of her life.

"You will have much suffering" was the warning given to the shepherds by the same Beautiful Lady who glorified the existence of Bernadette. But she also comforted them with the promise to crown their sufferings with a happiness, perfect and interminable in heaven.

True to her promise she led Jacinta into the presence of the Beatific Vision at the tender age of nine years and eleven months, nevermore to be separated from the company of the Lady who had chosen her for one of her own.

Clothed in white, with a ribbon of blue, in compliance with the wish of the little child, so that she might bear in death the colors of her beloved Lady, the body of Jacinta was taken to the neighboring Church of the Angels, which immediately became the center of a mighty pilgrimage of the faithful.

They all wished to see the "little angel," to touch her with religious articles which they henceforth would keep and revere as relics.

She lay on an open bier, with bloom of pristine health once again reddening her lips and cheeks, in solemn tranquility, and more beautiful than she had ever appeared in life. The people abandoned themselves to admiration and joy, and in some cases, to an almost frenzied enthusiasm, according to the testimony of those who had been delegated to keep watch beside the corpse. They also inform us, that although she died of a purulent disease, and the body was exposed to public veneration for three and one-half days, there emanated from the remains a perfume such as comes only from the most fragrant flowers, filling the air of the whole edifice. "Even the most incredulous were forced to admit its presence."

"It is the odor of sanctity," said the devout.

"It is the perfume of the Virgin," said others.

It was that same delightful fragrance that streamed three years previously from the branches stripped by the children from the tree in Valinhos, where the Virgin appeared, following their imprisonment.

Her precious body was placed in a leaden coffin and entombed in a private chapel belonging to the baronial family of Alvajazere, in the cemetery at Villanova de Ourem.

Fifteen years later, on September 13, 1935, a formal inspection was made of the corpse, which had been sprinkled with quick lime, as was the prescribed law at that time to treat bodies that had succumbed to the epidemic. The officials were astounded to find her features miraculously preserved and recognizable.

Today she lies in the humble cemetery of Fatima, next to her brother Francisco, in a tomb erected for them by the bishop of the diocese.

When Lucia received a photograph of the preserved body of her little cousin from the Prelate of Leiria, she thanked him in a letter from which we quote: "I am overflowing with joy at seeing once more the features of the most intimate little friend of my childhood. May God grant her the nimbus of sanctity—for the glory of the most Blessed Virgin."

PART SEVEN

Last Revelations

"Must I Remain Alone?"

Jacinta and Francisco had walked the way of the cross, and then—the path to heaven.

Shortly before she left Fatima for Lisbon, Jacinta, who had been only a silent witness in the apparitions, but now had become an impassioned herald of the message of Fatima, summoned Lucia to her bedside. Between sorrowful words of final farewell, in the grave and solemn manner of one who entrusts a sacred command and unburdens the heart of a compelling trust; with an authority and force of persuasion found only in the dying who are obsessed by a lofty ideal, she began, like a prophetess, to speak of the special mission that was reserved for the surviving cousin: "In a short while I shall go to heaven. You must remain here to make known the fact that the Lord wants to have established in the world the devotion to the Immaculate Heart of Mary. When the time comes for you to speak of these things, do not hide yourself. Say that God desires to be bountiful with His graces through the Heart of the Immaculate. Tell the people to ask her for these graces; and that the Sacred Heart of Jesus wants to be honored together with Mary's Immaculate Heart. Tell them that all mankind should plead the cause of peace with the Immaculate Heart, because the Lord has placed in her hands alone the peace of the whole world. Here in my breast, there is a burning fire of love for the Hearts of Jesus and Mary, and the flames of that love I would gladly spread to the hearts of others!"

Instead, the flame was extinguished. She died. Lucia, the eldest of the three children, was left alone on earth.

Tearfully she confesses: "What a sadness to find myself alone,"—deprived now of the exquisite friendship of her beloved companions. "In such a brief space of time I had lost my dear papa, then Francisco, and now, Jacinta! As soon as I found it possible, I ran to the Cabeco, and burying myself in the grotto, alone with God, I poured out my grief in a flood of tears.

"Coming down from the mount, everything reminded me of my dead companions: the stones we used for seats; the flowers that Jacinta loved so passionately; the valleys where we ran and played with the pure delights of paradise! As if doubting the reality of everything, and lost in distress, I came back to my aunt's house, and approaching Jacinta's room, began to call her name. Theresa, her sister, seeing me in this state of mind, stopped me, and brought me back to my senses by saying: 'Jacinta has gone from us—forever!'

"...For a long time my sadness increased, from day to day."

With a great effort she resigned herself to her loss.

Had she not asked the Lady, in the second apparition, when told of the coming separation from her cousins: "Must I remain here below *alone?*" And had not the Virgin assured her: "No, my child! You will suffer greatly, but do not be discouraged! I shall never forsake you! In my Immaculate Heart you shall find refuge and a way to lead you to God!"

Our Lady graciously pointed out to her the motive for this decree, outlining her future mission on earth, and assigning a role to her which, humanly speaking, was most disagreeable to one of her nature, and just the opposite of that which would have pleased her most—that is, to join Francisco and Jacinta immediately in that glorious abode of which she had had a mere glimpse in the apparitions.

"You shall remain here below for many years, because it is the will of Jesus that you are to be the instrument that shall make me better known and loved by mankind in the establishment of the devotion to my Immaculate Heart."

When the pilgrims now thronged to the Cova for the Feast of the Queen of May, 1920, and in the following months, they saw only one child instead of three. Modestly and devoutly she led them in the recitation of the rosary, and joyously they answered the beloved invocations. Then they began to miss her presence occasionally at the devotions. They would search for her at Aljustrel. She was not there either. Finally she disappeared completely.

Lucia informs us that there existed an intimate spiritual relationship between the seers and the rural Vicar of Ourem, the Reverend Faustine G. Ferreira, a man of singular talent and virtue. Because of his piety and devotion to the Blessed Virgin, he of all the clergy was the one most likely to comprehend the significance of the happenings in Fatima. From the time of the apparitions on, therefore, he had established communication with the three shepherds, who lived far remote from his daily ministry, which no one ever suspected as including the wondrous lives of the children. He was a godsend to Lucia now, in the hour of overwhelming grief and perplexity.

"He it was," Lucia reveals, "who strengthened us in our preservations of the secrets, and gave us spiritual instruction, showing us the various methods of pleasing God by little sacrifices. He would tell us, for example, that if we took pleasure in partaking of a certain food or delicacy, we could abstain from it or eat something less palatable, offering our abstention as a spiritual sacrifice to God, and with the same motive, that we could shorten or omit our amusements, shun or answer all interrogations, in a manner that seemed most pleasing to our Lord.

"We received much enlightenment from that venerable priest, and were pleased with our association with him."

From their first encounter, the good Father Faustine was able to read the heart of Lucia, and recognized in her the making of a great saint. All his efforts were directed to that eventuality.

"Keeping my spiritual welfare in mind," Lucia continues to reveal, "he extended his benevolence through the services of a pious widow named Emily, who came often to the Cova to pray. Passing our house frequently, she requested permission to take me away with her for a short while, and conducted me to the house of the Rural Vicar. There I enjoyed his hospitality, for three or four days, under the pretext of caring for his little niece. He spent many patient hours with me, pointing out the paths of virtue and guiding me with his wise counsel. Not knowing, hitherto, what spiritual direction meant, I can say that he was my first spiritual adviser. My memories of him are both sacred and grateful. How he could read souls from afar!"

Lucia's temporary absences were not enough. It was decided that she must be taken away at once from those places where she was the center of attraction and from the annoyances of indiscreet crowds. Even the privacy of her own home was continually being violated, and long since had ceased to be a safe refuge from the curiosity of visitors.

"We cannot endure it any longer," wailed the mother, Mary-Rose, at the height of the annoyances.

Fortunately, the bishop of Leiria recognized their difficulties and having counseled in secrecy with the two persons most intimately affected— Lucia and her mother—he prudently advised that the child move permanently to a place of safety and comparative comfort. She was to leave her native village and go to a distant place in utmost secrecy!

On the eve of her departure, May 15, 1921, Lucia made a last visit to the various scenes of her happiest days: to the chapel, to bid farewell to the blessed Lord in the tabernacle, to whom she had so often poured out her soul in silent conversation and whom she had so many times received into her soul in Holy Communion; to the cemetery, where she knelt and prayed for a long time at the tombs of her father and her saintly companion Francisco; to Valinhos and to the Cova, consecrated by the presence of the beautiful Lady, who had blessed her eyes and soul with the ineffable vision of her glory; up to Mount Cabeco, to the grotto, where the messenger of the Lord had appeared to the three, and fed them, miraculously, with the bread of angels from a chalice borne from paradise.

It was the month of Mary. The day was radiantly beautiful, and as Lucia went from one hallowed site to another, she remembered it was on just such a day as this, on the 13th of May, four years ago, that she was first blessed with the vision of the Virgin. Only two days ago she had rapturously celebrated the third anniversary of that glorious day in Fatima. And now on this, her last sorrowful pilgrimage of farewell, she had met a group of people up on the sacred mount, and they had stared at her, almost enviously, and sought to detain her that they might join her in prayer, although they realized that she was heavy of heart, and in a hurry.

It was growing dark when she arrived back home, in the little thicket behind the house. Moonlight fell on the white stones around the spring. She fell on her knees before "the Virgin's lamp" and rested her head against the top edge of the slab that covered the water. Among the shadows she almost felt the presence of her departed cousins, and she murmured to them a long, sad litany of farewells. Then she kissed the cold, white stones of the spring —one by one—as so many silent witnesses of bygone days of prayer and sacrifice, and of amusement; silent listeners to so many secrets that they confided to one another out of the purity of their hearts.... Backing away and gazing all about her, she softly cried: "Farewell, dear spring and lovely yard, where I often came to look into the firmament, to see the break of day and the coming of night, the countless stars, the wondrous dome of the skies...."

As she entered the house, she gave a start—the whole world seemed to crash in on her.

Two hours after midnight, while the whole village slept—even the members of her own household!—she and her mother and an uncle set out on the long journey prescribed for her.

The road went up through the Cova. In passing, she begged leave for one last visit to the chapel and to the little oak whereon the Virgin had stood in the visions.

There it was—what was left of it—a slender stem sticking up out of the earth; no branches, no foliage—a mere relic of a tree, slashed and bruised and despoiled by vandals.

She knelt for the last time on the very spot from which she had gazed into the eyes of God's holy Mother, and back to her memory came flooding all the events of those heavenly manifestations. Sighing and weeping, in a mixture of joy and sadness, she kissed the sacred ground, caressed the stump of the hallowed tree, then rose quietly and obediently, as someone in the party urged that they be on their way.

The faint light of daybreak came to brighten the road. As the cart rolled on, Lucia turned to gaze at the receding landscape, the land she loved so well, the land of so many delightful days as well as saddened hours. With a final wave of the hand in the direction of the Cova, she dropped her weary head and gave herself up, to weeping and silent prayer, until they reached Leiria, where she bade farewell—what a farewell!—to her mother.

On the 17th of May, she entered the Orphanage of Villar, in Oporto. It was an Institute for girls, directed by the Sisters of St. Dorothy. Accepted by the Mother Superior solely upon the recommendation of the Bishop of Leiria, with the understanding that she was to be treated as a "singular case," she was told that she must adhere to the following precepts: she must tell no one of her identity nor whence she came; she must never speak of the apparitions, nor mention a word about Fatima and its famous happenings; if anybody should ask from which province she came, she must answer simply that she came from the vicinity of Lisbon; her name, henceforth, was to be "Mary Dos Dores," i.e., Mary of the Dolors.

What a coincidence! "Mary of the Dolors!" As if the last four years, and the years to come, were summed up in her very name, for "dolors" meant "sorrows."

Lucia had the uncommon grace to immediately recognize the situation for what it was. She was to withdraw herself in silence and humility from the gaze and even the recognition of the world, that the Virgin of Fatima and her message might stand out prominently in her place, and in their intended sphere. She accepted peacefully every stipulation of her acceptance, preserving scrupulously the injunction of silence.

Like John the Baptizer who said, "Christ must increase, but I must decrease," the humble shepherdess of Aljustrel gave a paralleled expression: "I desire to be forgotten that Fatima may be known forever!"

As was to be expected, the news of Lucia's disappearance led to much curiosity throughout the land.

There was a great commotion in Fatima. There was an uproar on the part of both the benevolent and the malevolent. Especially among the women, the whisperers and the slanderers, much was made of the mysterious disappearance. Many were the importunities inflicted upon the child's family, the Dos Santos. But nobody seemed to know anything.

Talk and rumors spread beyond the confines of Fatima to the ever suspicioning ears of the enemy of old, the Administrator of Villanova, and once more he entered upon a role of terror. He commanded Mary-Rose into his august presence, and demanded "in the name of the law" that she reveal the whereabouts of her missing daughter. The brave mother, vigorous and prudent as ever, made answer:

"My daughter is where both she and I wish that she be! More than that I have nothing to reveal!"

Several years went by. She who as a child had feasted her mortal eyes on the celestial beauty and grace of God's holy Mother; she who had dominated the thousands upon thousands of pilgrims in the Cova, putting them on their knees in the mud in the pouring rain by a sweep of her arm at the approach of the vision, or directing their eyes to the most terrifying sight of a whirling, crashing sun in the sky with the mere lift of a finger—she was a child no longer.

The intervening years had been good to her; she had found peace at last.

Within the sheltering walls of the orphanage the desire had been born to dedicate herself wholly to God in the state of evangelical perfection. When first she spoke of it to the Mother Superior there, that worthy person had told her to wait awhile longer, that she was yet too young to settle such weighty matters. But as time went on, and the superior would ask her if she still entertained such holy thoughts, Lucia would say: "I never lose the thought and desire of becoming a nun! To give myself entirely to Jesus is the greatest desire of my heart!"

She entered the Novitiate established in Tuy, Spain, by the Portuguese Province of the Institute of the Sisters of St. Dorothy, after its expulsion from Portugal in 1910. She received the religious habit, and after two years of probation, on October 3, 1928, she made her first vows. Six years later, on the same date, she was accepted as a perpetual member of the Institute. The holocaust was perfected; the satisfaction completed.

The significant name applied to her in the orphanage was adopted for life, but to the sweet name of Mary was added her own, thus linking together into one splendid binomial in memory of bygone days the prime characters of the prodigies of Fatima: one heavenly, the other earthly. Her name now was Sister Mary-Lucia Dos Dores.

Now that she has attained peace and happiness, we realize that her "dolors," her tears and sufferings were indispensable for the consummation of the holocaust on the altar of sacrifice, that she might make fruitful her apostolate for the redemption of souls.

A Missionary of Mary's Immaculate Heart

From the book *Fatima*, authored by A ntero de Figueiredo, we quote an interesting passage in connection with the present life of Sister Lucia: "In an interview in which she was earnestly solicited for information by a person invested with the authority of investigating and learning the various revelations and confidences received by her in the apparitions at Fatima, she humbly and modestly made the following answer:

"I am in Fatima on the 13th of every month in which the Virgin appeared. Since I am not permitted to make the vigil during the Nocturnal Adoration, I use the time by projecting my spirit into Fatima, prostrating myself with the thousands of pilgrims before the exposed Sacrament. I pray for them and for myself, until my body here is completely reabsorbed. In the morning, at Mass in the Convent Chapel, I close my eyes, and spiritually I am back in Fatima, hearing Mass there, and there also, out in the open, I receive Communion along with the others.

"I recite the rosary with the community, but, in reality, my community is elsewhere: it is the crowds of pilgrims in the Cova da Iria. I stroll about recalling the happy days of the apparitions. Presently I hear the multitude singing the hymns as they march in procession.

"At the Mass of the Infirm, I ask God to have pity on all of them, whether sick of soul or of body, and also a blessing for myself.

"Before evening I am back home again in the convent."

The present state of the world, with its disruptions and confusion, with new hatreds and new sufferings arising from the merciless shifting and shuffling of entire nations, civil war and threats of another global war—the horizon does not look too favorable for the advent of a long era of peace—but God is good and merciful, and works in various ways to attain His ends.

For the moment, the triumph of the Lady of the Rosary seems obscured, but in the meantime we have the consolation of knowing that Sister Lucia—the hidden pledge of heaven's merciful interference—has been favored with additional visitations from on high, and that Mary is still interested in her wayward children on earth.

The Mistress of Novices one day sent Sister Lucia on an errand that took her out of the convent. When she returned, her superior noticed a look of pleasant surprise, of joy and remembrance upon her features. Curious to know the cause of her happiness the Mistress asked: "What has happened?"

Modestly lowering her eyes, Sister Lucia answered simply: "The Virgin appeared to me."

The community was asked one time to provide volunteers for a new convent that was to be established by the congregation in Africa. Sister Mary-Lucia, being professed at the time, immediately went to the Mother Provincial and generously offered her service.

"What reason have you for wishing to go?" the Mother Provincial asked her.

"I would like to be a missionary and work for the salvation of souls. It would be a delight to teach the catechism!"

The Mother Provincial was well acquainted with the religious humility of the applicant, but she realized, too, that heaven had other designs with her. She contented herself with saying: "No, not for the present. It is the will of our Lady that you sanctify yourself in some other manner. She herself will point it out to you."

Realizing that she had acted too impulsively and that the Superior was only testing her motives, Sister Lucia's face reddened as she humbly bowed her head in submission.

She was to be a missionary, of course, but in the wider field of the apostolate of Mary's Immaculate Heart. For this field she continued to prepare herself by an ever increasing holiness of life. In the ministry of souls every apostle must possess the light and the life of sanctity.

Lucia declared: "I love holiness that is simple, and full of cheerfulness; one that may be suffused in a smile. St. John Bosco says that melancholy is the 'eighth' capital sin!"

"Joy," as a noted English convert puts it, "is the overpowering secret of a Christian."

A Portuguese priest, visiting in Tuy, was given permission to celebrate the community Mass in the convent of the Sisters of St. Dorothy. Sister Mary-Lucia, who was sacristan at the time, was busy sorting and laying out the proper vestments when the stranger turned and whispered to her: "Would it be possible for me to see the famous

Sister Mary-Lucia of whom everybody speaks in
Portugal?"

"Famous?" asked the attendant.

"Yes. What does she look like?"

"She looks like any other sister—just like me!"

That is as far as the priest got in the satisfaction of his curiosity, and when he left, he did not
know that he had seen and spoken to Sister Mary-
Lucia herself.

It being decided that the whole community of
the Institute of St. Dorothy should be consecrated
to the Immaculate Heart of Mary at the very site of
the apparitions, the Mother Provincial summoned
Lucia and asked her if she wished to accompany
the other sisters on the grand pilgrimage, and thus
gain a visit to Fatima—the first, after so many
years!

Sister Mary-Lucia answered humbly and
simply: "I would go only if I were sent under an
order of obedience!"

The prudence of her judgment was recognized
and Sister Lucia stayed home, happy and content,
although filled with an overwhelming desire to see
once more the beloved and sacred scenes of her
childhood.

The little Spanish city of Tuy is separated
from Portugal by the river Minho, on the boundary line. As soon as they crossed the river, one
day, Sister Lucia and a companion sister met three
strangers.

"Are you Sisters of St. Dorothy from Tuy?"

"Yes!" Sister Lucia answered promptly.

"We go to visit Lucia, the seer of Fatima. She is in Spain, is she not?"

"No, at the present moment she is in Portugal!" corrected Sister Lucia, most naturally.

The strangers looked surprised and incredulous: "But if she were in Tuy, could we possibly get to see her? They say it is very difficult to get permission to see her."

"Certainly you could get to see her!"

"How?"

"By just looking at her, just as you are now looking at me!"

When they left, the two sisters laughed merrily at the expense of the unsuspecting strangers.

While others sought so assiduously to visit and talk to Sister Lucia, she went about her daily tasks and devotions in the convent quite naturally and unobserved by the community.

She has a great and lively faith. "I believe that in the sacred Host there is an invisible beauty, far surpassing anything I have ever seen. I believe much more readily in what I see through the eyes of faith than in what I saw through the eyes of the body. These can err; those, never!"

Her ideals are immense: "My desire is to live with Jesus, to possess Jesus, and to be happy with Jesus!"

At the same time she wishes to be unobserved: "Lord, hide me ever more and more!"

Very appropriately, Lucia's name signifies "light." It comes from the Latin, "lucere"—to shine, to brighten, and is indicative of her mission on earth. "Lucia"—by the light of her apostolic zeal and sanctity, a reverberation of "the Lady clothed with the sun"—is to irradiate a dark and sinful world, whose conscience is obscured by iniquity. "Lucia"—by her light—is to reflect the bounty of the messages of the Immaculate Virgin, the warm and vivifying rays which are to thaw and soften the hard, frozen hearts of an ungrateful and indifferent humanity.

We might profitably consider the life of this nun in a dual phase: the first would assume a similarity to that of St. Bernadette Soubirous. Like the seer of Lourdes, she entered the convent as a lay sister, to live a life of simplicity and humility, occupying herself with the ordinary tasks of the community, and with filial piety towards our Blessed Lady; by a more forceful attraction to the Sacrament of the Altar; by an indefatigable ardor in the propagation of the devotion to the holy rosary as a means of salvation.

In the second phase, she reminds us of Saint Margaret Mary Alacoque, the great Apostle of the Sacred Heart, who received and propagated the Great Promise contained in the devotion to the Sacred Heart of Jesus.

Sister Mary-Lucia's mission is to perform an identical service for the Immaculate Heart of Mary.

The authoritative call for the spread of this devotion springs from the apparitions of June and July, 1917, in which our Lady instructed Lucia to reveal to us and to promote this devotion, together with the practice of honoring her on the First Saturday of the month.

These are our Lady's words: "It is the will of Jesus that you remain here on earth much longer" —(longer than Francisco and Jacinta—"in order that through you my Immaculate Heart may become better known and loved. Then you too shall be taken into paradise!"

But how was she to promote this devotion if she received from her superiors a rigorous injunction of silence?... She remained silent! It was not for her to decide. Perhaps God's hour had not yet struck!

It was December 17, 1927, ten years after the apparitions. The modest seer, at that time a novice, was in the chapel of the convent, in adoration before the holy tabernacle. She was asking our Lord how she was to satisfy the demand of her confessor that she put to writing the various revelations that she had received, insofar as they were secrets entrusted to her by the Blessed Virgin.

Clearly she heard these words, as Jesus spoke to her assuringly: "My daughter, do as you have been bidden. Write whatever the Blessed Virgin has confided to you concerning the devotion to the Immaculate Heart of my Mother—but on the remainder you may continue to be silent."

Obedient as always, she now submitted to the demands of her spiritual adviser and wrote: "On June 13, the Virgin consolingly assured me that she would never abandon me, and that her Immaculate Heart would always be my refuge and lead me finally to God.

"With this promise the Blessed Virgin disjoined her own hands that had been folded, and for a second time there flashed over us a mysterious light, in which we seemed to be immersed in God. One penciled ray from those hands pierced toward heaven, and the other one was projected towards the earth. The first suffused the figures of Francisco and Jacinta, the other, my own.

"Then, in the right hand of the apparition we saw a heart, encircled with thorns, that bruised and pierced it on every side. We recognized in it the heart of the Immaculate Mary, wounded by the many sins of humanity, and suppliant of penance and reparation.

"It seems to me," Lucia writes, "that on that day was given to us the infusion of this light to comprehend and to be attracted to the heart of Mary, just as, on other occasions, it was the intention to enlighten us and to develop in us a love and knowledge of God and the Blessed Trinity. From then on we nourished a most ardent affection for them in our hearts."

It was eight years since that glorious vision—and Lucia was eighteen years of age. She was not yet a religious, nor a novice. She was yet on probation.

On December 10, 1925, the document informs us, our Lady appeared to her in a brilliant emanence of light that sprang from her bosom, a furnace of flame, exposing a wounded, transfixed heart, the token of her maternal love. By her side was the Infant Jesus, standing on a luminous cloud. Pointing to His Mother's breast, He exhorted Lucia: "Have compassion with the holy sweetness of this heart, so continuously crushed by man's ingratitude, with none to console it by acts of reparation."

Then the eyes of the Virgin fell on her with a look of infinite tenderness, and she communicated to her the Great Revelation of her Immaculate Heart in the words destined to become some of the greatest in the annals of Mariology, giving universal joy, devotion and enthusiasm:

"Behold, my child, this heart encircled with thorns, and bleeding incessantly because of the sins of blasphemy and ingratitude of man. You, at least, must seek to comfort me!

"And let it be known to the whole world that I promise to help, at the hour of death, with all the graces needed for eternal salvation, all those who, on the first Saturday of the month, for five consecutive months, shall confess, receive Holy Communion, recite a third of the rosary, and keep company with me by devoting fifteen minutes of their time to the meditation of the mysteries of the rosary, with the intention of offering me reparation for the sins committed against my Immaculate Heart."

This is the last of the Revelations of Fatima: a most extraordinary favor, not conceded because of any pre-existing or possible merit of ours, but rather out of a stupendous, unexpected manifestation of the profound love of our celestial Mother.

It is known as the "Great Promise of the Immaculate Heart of Mary!"

And justly so, because of the numerous, consoling promises that Our Lady of Mercy has made in the course of all her apparitions to privileged souls, this one exceeds them all. In the value and immensity of this great gift, we must consider it a worthy parallel to the Great Promise of the Sacred Heart of Jesus.

As the heart of Jesus is a "burning furnace of charity," so the heart of Mary is a flaming furnace of compassion and mercy for sinners. As Jesus thirsted for souls and manifested His love in the work of Redemption, so His Mother thirsts for souls and came down from heaven to tell us through three little innocent shepherds that the floodgates of divine Mercy are wide open for those who will take refuge in her Immaculate Heart.

It is heaven's desire, and for us a necessity, that we comprehend the deep significance of this revelation: its purpose, its conditions, the spirit that must animate us in the devotion, and its finality.

In the first place, it may seem to some people, that in the practice of this devotion, the benefits are entirely out of proportion to the effort involved. There is a disproportion, indeed, but no more than that which exists between the visible sign of a sacrament and its spiritual effect. In striking a balance between cause and effect we must never ignore the intervention of God's holy will, and the bountiful mercy of the Immaculate Heart of Mary.

But why is the fulfillment of this extraordinary promise dependent upon five Saturdays and a few conditions? Is there not a suspicion of artificiality and superstition contained in these stipulations? Not at all! To such objectors, and to all the faithful who ask most legitimately whether the Great Promise be an authentic revelation of the Mother of God, we answer that it is a historical certitude, really authentic and approved by the Church.

As previously mentioned, it was communicated, years ago, by Lucia to her confessor who, in turn, notified the proper ecclesiastical authorities. The Church, cautious and reserved as always, instituted a diligent, severe and minute examination of the celestial message, and not only did she not disapprove of it, but confirmed it in its entirety, and permitted it to be told to the faithful.

It was published for the first time on September 13, 1939, in Fatima, with the Imprimatur of His Excellency, Jose'-Alves Correia da Silva, Bishop of Leiria.

In that same year, the "Official Manual of the Pilgrimages to Fatima" and the "Official Calendar of the Sanctuary" quoted the words of the Great Promise, and explained the conditions connected with its fulfillment. We extract from it the following passage: "It is our Lady herself, who, in our own times, has deigned to initiate the devotion of the Five First Saturdays, to the end that reparation be made for outrages committed against her by ungrateful souls.... This devotion was revealed to Sister Lucia by the Blessed Virgin...."

By this statement duly sanctioned, we are permitted to speak freely of the revelation, with all the sincerity and conviction of our minds. We are not the first to do so. For example, the Vatican Radio announced it to the world as soon as the Great Promise was approved; and on the first Saturday of every month it devoted a quarter hour to the meditation of the mysteries of the rosary for the benefit of those who were practicing the devotion.

Moreover, it may be remarked, that the desires of the Blessed Virgin, as expressed by Sister

Mary-Lucia, *sanctioned and confirmed* a devotion that has been in existence since the time of the French Revolution, and has been confirmed by ecclesiastical approval. In fact, Pope Pius X, in a Decree of June 13, 1912, granted a plenary indulgence to all those who on the first Saturday of every month, having confessed their sins and received Holy Communion, performed certain acts of devotion in honor of the Immaculate Virgin, in a spirit of reparation and praying for the intention of the Holy Father.

Our Lady of Fatima blessed and approved of the above practice, and in the devotion of the Five First Saturdays, she simply specifies the conditions and the particular manner in which we are to honor her in order to gain the benefit of the Great Promise.

Another fact appears evident, and this is, that the devotion of the Five First Saturdays bears the same relation to the Mother of God as do the Nine First Fridays to the Sacred Heart of Jesus. These two devotions should be parallel, for it is manifestly the divine will that they should be so, although the former is completed in five months, whereas the other requires nine.

The Postulates of Her Promise

The "Great Promise of the Immaculate Heart of Mary" is necessarily tied to the performance of the following determinant acts, upon which it is essentially conditioned:

1. **Confession**—This is necessary on all five First Saturdays. It is intended that the confession be made properly, that is, with sorrow and sincerity, after a thorough examination of conscience. Any doubt as to upon which day we should confess was removed for us by Sister Mary-Lucia, who received her instruction in an apparition of the Infant Jesus, on February 15, 1926, wherein she was encouraged to the propagation of this devotion, no matter what obstacles should intervene. She tells us that it is sufficient if we confess within eight days preceding or following each First Saturday, so long as we are in the state of grace when we receive Communion. Generally, the confession for a First Friday suffices for the First Saturday.

2. **Holy Communion**—We must be in the state of grace. That is sufficient. No special fervor is required, but everyone should strive to attain to the greatest fervor possible in accord with his own capability. Thoughtful preparation for the coming of the Eucharistic Lord, and heartfelt gratitude for the favor received are unmistakable signs of a good Communion. Let us not forget that our Communion is to be one of reparation, for the sins of

blasphemy and all other offenses against the Immaculate Heart of Mary.

3. **Recitation of a third part of the rosary**— The rosary! the perfect prayer, and most dear to the Heart of Mary! The weapon that wins every battle! The chain that binds us to her, and leads us to salvation!

We may meditate, while reciting it, on the Joyful, the Sorrowful, or the Glorious Mysteries, just as we please, repeatedly or alternately.

4. **Fifteen minutes of meditation on the mysteries**—Meditation is the soul of the rosary; in fact, it is the motive for every prayer, which must spring from the interior and permeate our whole being. The Virgin of Fatima specifies—for the first time, perhaps in the history of her terrestrial visitations—fifteen minutes of reflection, to center our minds on Jesus, the Truth, the Way, and the Life; and on the Gospel.

This concentration of the mind on a particular subject may be difficult for some of the devout, but it is an obstacle that can and must be overcome by putting ourselves into the proper disposition for prayer. And what is prayer? Is it not a lifting of the heart and the mind to God, in love and adoration?

To simplify the meditation, we may dwell on all the fifteen mysteries (one minute of reflection on each), or consider a few of them only. Even one mystery could be chosen by those who intended to repeat the Five First Saturdays Devotion in succession, thus, in time, completing the meditation of the whole series of fifteen.

It is, of course, permitted to unite the prescribed recitation of a third part of the rosary with the meditation. In this case, as each single mystery is announced, we may stop and dwell in thought upon it for a few minutes, then proceed with the recitation of the Our Father and the Hail Marys.

There are several booklets with short but practical meditations on all the mysteries of the rosary. To facilitate the meditation required by the Immaculate Heart, it is suggested that these meditations be read slowly, to obtain the proper effect and to be accomplished with a definite purpose.*

The requirement of meditation may be satisfied by listening on that day to a sermon, or by reading a religious book or treatise on the subject of the mysteries of the rosary.

Therefore, the meditation and the recitation of the rosary may be united or separated, so long as both are performed in deference to the will of the Blessed Virgin.

We may practice this devotion publicly or privately, in church or at home, at any hour convenient for us, and according to one's own inclinations, never forgetting the injunction, or the purpose, of keeping company with the Immaculate Heart of Mary as a loving child would do with its own mother.

---

*Ten Series of Meditations on the Mysteries of the Rosary, by Rev. John Ferraro, published by the Daughters of St. Paul;

The Great Promise of Our Lady of Fatima, 56 pages — PM0830.

For children: My Rosary coloring book   — CH0400. Order from addresses inside back cover. Please use item number when ordering.

5. **On the first Saturday of the month**—This devotion may not be transferred arbitrarily to some other day of the week. We must receive Holy Communion, recite the rosary and make the quarter hour meditation on the first Saturday of the month. This condition is essential and immutable. Not even a confessor has the faculty of changing it, nor may the sick or infirm be dispensed from this condition.

6. **For five consecutive months**—These are clear words, and mean just what they say. There must be no interruption in the sequence, no matter how involuntary. Once the series is broken for any cause, we must begin all over again. The reason for this is obvious. When accepting a gift, one naturally submits to the will of the donor, and willingly accedes to the conditions governing the presentation.

7. **"With the intention of offering me reparation"**—In a spirit of filial love, humility and contrition for our own sins, we are to console the Immaculate Heart, saddened by the coldness, the ingratitude of so many souls, and the offenses of all mankind. Herein is contained the aim, the whole purpose and final cause of the devotion. Together with the will to perform all the other requirements in order to obtain the Great Promise, it is sufficient that this intention be *virtual*, that is, being formulated expressly, once and for all, at the beginning of the devotion, and that it is not revoked. It is not necessary that it be actual, that is, it need not be renewed on each First Saturday, although it is advisable to renew it.

Undoubtedly, if one were to have an intention opposed to the one required—for example, if one were to practice this devotion in order to abandon oneself later to a life of sin—that person certainly could not claim the benefit of a happy death. That would be a perverse intention, and an abuse of the bountiful mercy of the Immaculate Heart.

It is ardently recommended, and most pleasing to the Heart of the Immaculate Mother, that everyone repeat over and over, throughout life, the practice of the Devotion of the Five First Saturdays, to honor God's Mother and to make ourselves worthy of her special favor.

By the power of example we shall bring others, too, to a knowledge of the reparation due to the Immaculate Heart of Mary on the first Saturday, and aid in the work of her Son's redemption of sinners. Let us remember, that "to save a soul," St. Ambrose declares, "is a work greater than creation, more glorious than to raise the dead. It is the assurance of everlasting life."

"Have you saved a soul?" asks St. Augustine. "You have predestined your own!"

The Virgin said to Lucia: "To those who will practice this devotion to my Immaculate Heart, I promise eternal salvation. They shall be my favorite souls of God and be like choice flowers placed by me before His throne."

PART EIGHT

Queen of Peace

Consecration of the World to Mary

On Saturday, October 13, 1942, at the solemn close of the memorable celebration of the Jubilee of the apparitions of Fatima, Pope Pius XII, who had become a bishop at the same hour and on the same day that our Lady first had appeared in the Cova—the suffering and weeping Pope in the vision of the Great Secret, announced in a radio message to the world in general, but particularly to Portugal, the "Land of Mary": "Today, in the fourth year of war, we are saddened by the extent of the conflict; today, more than ever, our sole trust is in God, and in the Mediatrix before the divine throne, whom our predecessor—Benedict XV—in the first world-conflict invoked as the Queen of Peace. We supplicate her again, on this occasion, for she alone can help us"—(Note the almost literal repetition of the words of the Virgin in the third apparition)—"Mary, whose maternal heart was so solicitous for the disasters heaped upon your country and so wonderfully delivered it from them; Mary, who moved to pity by the vision of so much suffering that divine Justice has laid upon the earth, has anticipated our desires and shown us the way to safety by prayer and penance; Mary will not refuse us her affection nor the efficacy of her protection!"

The Holy Father spoke in accents of extreme anxiety. Every pause was but a suspension of his sorrow.

Then followed a sudden change to a canticle of exaltation:

"Queen of the Most Holy Rosary, Help of Christians, Refuge of Mankind, triumphant in all battles for God! We, your suppliants, prostrate ourselves at your throne, confident that we shall obtain mercy and receive grace, the needed assistance and protection, during the calamities of these days, not indeed by our own merits, of which we presume nothing, but solely through the immense goodness of your maternal heart.

"To you and to your Immaculate Heart, we, the common father of the vast Christian family, we, the Vicar of Him to whom was given all power in heaven and on earth,' and from whom we have received the care of so many souls redeemed by His blood; to you and to your Immaculate Heart in this tragic hour of human history, we commit, we entrust, we consecrate, not only the Holy Church, the Mystical Body of your Jesus, which suffers and bleeds in so many places and is afflicted in so many ways, but also the entire world torn by violent discord, scorched in a fire of hate, victim of its own iniquities.

"Be moved to pity in the face of so many material and moral disasters, by so many afflictions which agonize fathers and mothers, innocent babes! Be moved to compassion in view of so many lives cut off in the very flowering of youth, so many bodies mangled by the horrible slaughter, so many tortured and afflicted souls, so many in danger of eternal ruin!

"You, O Mother of Mercy, obtain for us peace from God! and above all obtain those graces which can convert human hearts in an instant, those graces which prepare for, promote and insure peace! Queen of Peace, pray for us and grant to this war-stricken world the peace which the nations desire: peace in the truth, in the justice and in the charity of Christ. Grant to us a cessation of this conflict and true peace of soul, that in the tranquillity of restored order, the kingdom of God may be spread.

"Extend your protection to unbelievers and to them who still stand in the shadow of death. Grant to them peace. May the Sun of truth dawn in their lives that they may join with us before Him who alone is Savior of the world and repeat these words: 'Glory to God in the highest and peace on earth to men of good will' (Luke 2:14).

"To the peoples separated by error or discord, and especially to those who profess special devotion to you and among whom there was once not a home where your venerated icon was not honored (today perhaps hidden and awaiting better days), grant peace and lead them back to the one fold of Christ under the one and true Shepherd.

"Obtain peace and complete liberty for the Holy Church of God. Check the inundating flood of neopaganism and all its materialism. Arouse in the faithful the love of purity, the practice of the Christian life, and apostolic zeal in order that the people who serve God may increase in merit and in number.

"Finally, just as the Church and the entire human race were consecrated to the Heart of your Jesus, because by placing in Him every hope, it may be for them a token and pledge of victory and salvation; so, henceforth, they are perpetually consecrated to you, to your Immaculate Heart, O our Mother and Queen of the world, in order that your love and protection may hasten the triumph of the kingdom of God. And may all peoples at peace among themselves and with God proclaim you blessed and intone with you throughout the entire world the eternal 'Magnificat' of glory, love and adoration of the Heart of Jesus, in whom alone they can find truth, love and peace."

This constitutes one of the most sublime acts in the pontificate of Pius XII, who, the following May, again exhorted the faithful to dedicate themselves to the Immaculate Heart in supplication for the needs of the human race and for the establishment of a just and lasting peace.

Two years later, Pius XII decreed the Feast of the Immaculate Heart of Mary, which is now celebrated on the Saturday following the feast of the Sacred Heart of Jesus.

In early April of 1948, Lucia entered the cloister of the Carmelite Order in Coimbra. Her name was now Sister Mary of the Immaculate Heart.

Prayer Intentions at Fatima*

The text of homily of Pope Paul VI at 50th Anniversary Celebration of the Fatima Apparitions is presented in full.

Tão grande é
May 13, 1967

Great is our desire to honor the Blessed Virgin Mary, Christ's Mother and therefore the Mother of God. Great is our confidence in her benevolence toward the holy Church and toward our apostolic mission. Great is our need for her intercession with Christ, her divine Son. For these reasons we have come as a lowly and trustful pilgrim to this blessed sanctuary. Here today we are celebrating the 50th anniversary of the apparitions at Fatima, and the 25th anniversary of the consecration of the world to the Immaculate Heart of Mary.

CONCERN FOR ALL MEN

It is a pleasure to be here with you, beloved brothers and sons, to join with you in professing our devotion to Mary, to associate you with our prayer. In this way our common veneration may be more public and more filial, and our plea may gain more ready acceptance.

We extend a greeting to all of you here present —in particular, to the citizens of this illustrious na-

---

*Reprinted with permission from *The Pope Speaks,* vol. 12, no. 12, Spring, 1967, Washington, D.C. 20017.

tion which in its long history has given the Church many great and holy men and a pious, hard-working people. We greet all you pilgrims who have come from near and far, and all the members of the Catholic Church in Rome and around the world who are spiritually present at this altar with us. Greetings to you all. We are here to celebrate Holy Mass with you and for you. We are united together here, as children of one family, around our heavenly Mother, so that during the Holy Sacrifice we may achieve closer and more salvific communion with Christ, our Lord and Savior.

We do not want to exclude anyone from this spiritual remembrance, because it is our wish that everyone share in the graces we are now going to implore from heaven. All of you have a place in our heart: our brother bishops, priests, men and women religious who have consecrated yourselves to Christ in total love; all Christian families; all you beloved lay people who wish to join forces with the clergy in extending the kingdom of God; all you young people and children whom we always want to have near us; all you who are weary and afflicted, all you who weep and suffer hardship, knowing full well that Christ calls you to His side to associate you with His redeeming passion and to give you comfort.

Our gaze turns also to all Christians who are not Catholics but who are our brothers through Baptism. We mention them with the hope of full communion with them in the unity that the Lord desires. And we also turn to the whole world. We do not want to set any limits to our love; in this moment we extend it to all mankind, to every government and to every nation of the earth.

PRAYER FOR THE CHURCH

You are aware of the special intentions which we wish to make the emblem of this pilgrimage. We shall recall them here, so that they may inspire our prayer and enlighten all who are listening to us.

The first intention is the Church: the one, holy, catholic and apostolic Church. As we have said, we wish to pray for its internal peace. The Ecumenical Council awakened many energies within the Church. It opened up broader perspectives in the whole area of Church doctrine. It has called all the Church's sons to a clearer awareness, a closer collaboration, and a more active apostolate. We earnestly hope that this beneficial and profound renewal will be carried on and further developed.

POTENTIALLY DISRUPTIVE ENERGIES

What a shame it would be if some arbitrary interpretation, not authorized by the Church's magisterium, were to turn this spiritual renewal into a disruptive force which would undermine the Church's traditional constitutional structure; a force which would replace the theology of the great authentic teachers with new partisan ideologies that would try to exclude from the norm of faith everything which modern thought—often lacking the light of reason—does not understand and accept; a force which would convert the apostolic concern of redeeming charity into base acquiescence to the negative qualities of the secular mentality and the way of the world. Our attempt to draw all men together would be a vain effort indeed if the Church did not offer, to our separated Christian brothers and to the rest of humanity who are not of our faith, the patrimony of truth and charity in its full authenticity and its original splendor—the patrimony which the Church guards and distributes.

We want to pray to Mary for a living Church, an authentic Church, a united Church, a holy Church. We wish to pray together with you that the hopes and energies aroused by the Council may bring us an abundant outpouring of the fruits of the Holy Spirit. He is the source of an authentic Christian life and we celebrate His feast tomorrow, the day of Pentecost. His fruits are listed by Saint Paul: "charity, joy, peace, patience, kindness, goodness, faith, modesty, continency" (Gal. 5:22-23).

It is our desire to offer a prayer that worship of God will maintain its priority in the world, today and forever; that His law will shape the conscience and the conduct of modern man. Faith in God is humanity's guiding light, and it should not be extinguished in the hearts of men. On the contrary, it should burn brighter under the stimulus provided by science and progress.

This line of thought motivates and animates our prayer, but in this moment it also makes us think of those countries where religious freedom is, for all practical purposes, suppressed; where rejection of God is fostered as if it represented the truth of a new age and the liberation of the populace.

The truth is quite different, however. Let us pray for these nations. Let us pray for our fellow believers in these countries, that God's inner power may sustain them and that genuine civil liberty may be granted to them.

PRAYER FOR PEACE

Now let us move on to the second intention that motivates this pilgrimage: the world, world peace. As you know, since the Council there has been a growing awareness of the Church's mission to the world, her mission of service and love. You know that the world is at a stage where great transformations are taking place, where enormous and wondrous progress is being made, where the riches of the earth and of the universe are being discovered and tapped. Yet you also can see that the world is not happy or tranquil.

WORLD IN DANGER

The first cause of this unrest resides in the fact that it is difficult to establish harmony, to insure peace. Everything seems to push the world toward brotherhood and unity; and yet we find terrifying and unabating conflicts in the heart of humanity. Humanity's present situation in history is made critical by two principal factors: man possesses a huge arsenal of frighteningly lethal weapons, but his moral progress does not keep pace with his scientific and technical progress. Furthermore, a large part of humanity is still enmeshed in hunger and poverty, while at the same time it experiences a growing and discomforting awareness of its own needs and of the prosperity of others. That is why we say that the world is in danger. That is why we have come to the feet of the Queen of Peace to plead for peace, the gift which only God can grant us.

AN APPEAL TO ALL MEN

Yes, peace is a gift from God. It requires His beneficial, merciful and mysterious intervention. But His gift is not always a miraculous one. It is a gift which works its wonders in the recesses of men's hearts, and hence it is a gift requiring ready acceptance and cooperation on our part. And so, after directing our prayer to heaven, we direct it to men all over the world. In this singular moment we say to them: Prove yourselves worthy of God's gift of peace! Be truly men! Be good, be prudent! Open your hearts and give thought to the good of the whole world! Be generous! Try to see that your prestige and interests are not opposed to those of others, but rather are one with theirs! Do not dwell upon schemes of destruction and death, of violence and revolution! Think rather about projects of mutual aid and joint collaboration!

Men of the world, consider the gravity and the grandeur of this moment, which could well be decisive for this generation and the generations to come! Begin again to draw together with the intention of building a new world, a world of real human beings, which cannot be fashioned unless God is the sun that shines on its horizon. Hear in our lowly and tremulous voice the echo of Christ's own words: "Blessed are the meek, for they shall possess the earth; blessed are the peacemakers, for they shall be called children of God."

You can see, dear sons and brothers listening to us, the drama and awesomeness that surround the world and its fortunes, as we have pictured it. It is a panorama which our Lady opens up to us, a scene which we contemplate with frightened but ever trustful eyes. It is a scene that we shall always approach as our Lady told us to approach it—with prayer and penance. That we pledge! May it record no more incidents of conflict, tragedy and catastrophe, but rather the conquests made by love and the victories won by peace.

Rosary: So Rich, So Simple

On Sunday, October 29, before the recitation of the Angelus in St. Peter's Square, Pope John Paul II delivered the following address.

Dear brothers and sisters,

Here we are again, meeting as we did a week ago to recite the Angelus together. This week has passed quickly, rich in important meetings and visits.

Today, the last Sunday of October, I wish to draw your attention to the rosary. In fact, throughout the whole Church, October is the month dedicated to the rosary.

The rosary is my favorite prayer. A marvelous prayer! Marvelous in its simplicity and in its depth. In this prayer we repeat many times the words that the Virgin Mary heard from the Archangel, and from her kinswoman Elizabeth. The whole Church joins in these words. It can be said that the rosary is, in a certain way, a prayer-commentary on the last chapter of the Constitution *Lumen gentium* of Vatican II, a chapter which deals with the wonderful presence of the Mother of God in the mystery of Christ and the Church.

In fact, against the background of the words "Ave Maria" there pass before the eyes of the soul the main episodes in the life of Jesus Christ. They are composed altogether of the joyful, sorrowful and glorious mysteries, and they put us in living communion with Jesus through—we could say—His Mother's heart.

At the same time our heart can enclose in these decades of the rosary all the facts that make up the life of the individual, the family, the nation, the Church and mankind. Personal matters and those of one's neighbor, and particularly of those who are closest to us, who are dearest to us. Thus in the simple prayer of the rosary beats the rhythm of human life.

During the last few weeks I have had the opportunity to meet many persons, representatives of various nations and of different environments as well as of various Christian Churches and communities. I wish to assure you that I have not failed to translate these relations into the language of the rosary prayer, in order that everyone might find himself at the heart of the prayer which gives a full dimension to everything.

In these last weeks both I and the Holy See have had numerous proofs of good will from people in the whole world. I wish to translate my gratitude into decades of the rosary in order to express it in prayer, as well as in the human manner; in this prayer so simple and so rich.

Yesterday afternoon I went down to the crypt of the Vatican Basilica to celebrate Mass for the month's mind of my predecessor, Pope John Paul I; and yesterday—as you well know—there occurred also the twentieth anniversary of the election of Pope John XXIII, whose paternal figure is ever alive in the hearts of the faithful.

John XXIII was a Pope who loved much and who was intensely loved. Let us remember him in prayer, and above all, let us seek to put into practice the precious legacy of the teachings he left us with his word, with his commitment of fidelity to tradition and of "aggiornamento," with his life, and with his holy death.

Now, let us recite together the Angelus.

The Mother in Whom
We Trust

*From Pope John Paul II's first encyclical,
"Redemptor Hominis."*

When, therefore, at the beginning of the new
pontificate I turn my thoughts and my heart to the
Redeemer of man, I thereby wish to enter and pen-
etrate into the deepest rhythm of the Church's life.
Indeed, if the Church lives her life, she does so
because she draws it from Christ, and He always
wishes but one thing, namely that we should have
life and have it abundantly (cf. Jn. 10:10). This
fullness of life in Him is at the same time for man.
Therefore the Church, uniting herself with all the
riches of the mystery of the Redemption, becomes
the Church of living people, living because given
life from within by the working of "the Spirit of
truth" (Jn. 16:13) and visited by the love that
the Holy Spirit has poured into our hearts (cf.
Rom. 5:5). The aim of any service in the Church,
whether the service is apostolic, pastoral, priestly
or episcopal, is to keep up this dynamic link between the mystery of the Redemption and every
man.

If we are aware of this task, then we seem to
understand better what it means to say that the
Church is a mother and also what it means to say
that the Church always, and particularly at our
time, has need of a Mother. We owe a debt of

special gratitude to the Fathers of the Second Vatican Council, who expressed this truth in the Constitution *Lumen gentium* with the rich Mariological doctrine contained in it. Since Paul VI, inspired by that teaching, proclaimed the Mother of Christ "Mother of the Church," and that title has become known far and wide, may it be permitted to his unworthy successor to turn to Mary as Mother of the Church at the close of these reflections which it was opportune to make at the beginning of his papal service. Mary is Mother of the Church because, on account of the eternal Father's ineffable choice and due to the Spirit of Love's special action, she gave human life to the Son of God, "for whom and by whom all things exist" (Heb. 2:10) and from whom the whole of the People of God receives the grace and dignity of election. Her Son explicitly extended His Mother's maternity in a way that could easily be understood by every soul and every heart by designating, when He was raised on the cross, His beloved disciple as her son (cf. Jn. 19:26). The Holy Spirit inspired her to remain in the Upper Room, after our Lord's ascension, recollected in prayer and expectation, together with the apostles, until the day of Pentecost, when the Church was to be born in visible form, coming forth from darkness (cf. Acts 1:14; 2). Later, all the generations of disciples, of those who confess and love Christ, like the apostle John, spiritually took this Mother to their own homes (cf. Jn. 19:27), and she was thus included in the history of salvation and in the Church's mission from the very beginning, that is from the moment of the Annunciation. Accordingly, we who form today's generation of disciples of Christ all wish to unite ourselves with her in a special way. We do so with all our attachment to our ancient tradition and also with full respect and love for the members of all the Christian communities.

We do so at the urging of the deep need of faith, hope and charity. For if we feel a special need, in this difficult and responsible phase of the history of the Church and of mankind, to turn to Christ, who is Lord of the Church and Lord of man's history on account of the mystery of the Redemption, we believe that nobody else can bring us as Mary can into the divine and human dimension of this mystery. Nobody has been brought into it by God Himself as Mary has. It is in this that the exceptional character of the grace of the divine Motherhood consists. Not only is the dignity of this Motherhood unique and unrepeatable in the history of the human race, but Mary's participation, due to this maternity, in God's plan for man's salvation through the mystery of the Redemption is also unique in profundity and range of action.

We can say that the mystery of the Redemption took shape beneath the heart of the Virgin of Nazareth when she pronounced her "fiat." From then on, under the special influence of the Holy Spirit, this heart, the heart of both a virgin and a mother, has always followed the work of her Son and has gone out to all those whom Christ has embraced and continues to embrace with inexhaustible love. For that reason her heart must also have the inexhaustibility of a mother. The special characteristic of the motherly love that the Mother of God inserts in the mystery of the Redemption and the life of the Church finds expression in its exceptional closeness to man and all that happens to him. It is in this that the mystery of the Mother consists. The Church, which looks to her with altogether special love and hope, wishes to make this mystery her own in an ever deeper manner. For in this the Church also recognizes the way for her daily life, which is each person.

The Father's eternal love, which has been manifested in the history of mankind through the Son whom the Father gave, "that whoever believes in him should not perish but have eternal life" (Jn. 3:16), comes close to each of us through this Mother and thus takes on tokens that are of more easy understanding and access by each person. Consequently, Mary must be on all the ways for the Church's daily life. Through her maternal presence the Church acquires certainty that she is truly living the life of her Master and Lord and that she is living the mystery of the Redemption in all its life-giving profundity and fullness. Likewise the Church, which has struck root in many varied fields of the life of the whole of present-day humanity, also acquires the certainty and, one could say, the experience of being close to man, to each person, of being each person's Church, the Church of the People of God.

Faced with these tasks that appear along the ways for the Church, those ways that Pope Paul VI clearly indicated in the first encyclical of his pontificate, and aware of the absolute necessity of all these ways and also of the difficulties thronging them, we feel all the more our need for a profound link with Christ. We hear within us, as a resounding echo, the words that He spoke: "Apart from me you can do nothing" (Jn. 15:5). We feel not only the need but even a categorical imperative for great, intense and growing prayer by all the Church. Only prayer can prevent all these great succeeding tasks and difficulties from becoming a source of crisis and make them instead the occasion and, as it were, the foundation for ever more mature achievements on the People of God's march towards the Promised Land in this stage of history approaching the end of the second millennium. Accordingly, as I end this meditation with a warm and humble call to prayer, I wish the Church to devote herself to this prayer, together with Mary the Mother of Jesus (cf. Acts 1:14), as the apostles and disciples of the Lord did in the Upper Room in Jerusalem after His ascension (cf. Acts 1:13). Above all, I implore Mary, the heavenly Mother of the Church, to be so good as to devote herself to this prayer of humanity's new advent, together with us who make up the Church, that is to say the Mystical Body of her only Son. I hope that through this prayer we shall be able to receive the Holy Spirit coming upon us (cf. Acts 1:8) and thus become Christ's witnesses "to the end of the earth" (cf. Acts 1:8), like those who went forth from the Upper Room in Jerusalem on the day of Pentecost.

A "Pilgrim" with the Pilgrims to Fatima

Pope's John Paul II's letter to the Bishop of Leiria, for the pilgrimage to Fatima on May 13, 1979.

To my venerable brother Alberto Cosme do Amaral, Bishop of Leiria (Portugal)

On next May 13, another great pilgrimage will be made to the sanctuary of Fatima, the program of which I was glad to know. For I am complying in this simple way with the desire you thought right to express to me that the new Successor of St. Peter, in the first year of his pontificate, should be present spiritually among the many pilgrims from Portugal and from all over the world who will gather in that blessed place.

In harmony, therefore, with this prayerful assembly, I cordially desire to wish pastors, priests, men and women religious, and beloved faithful, pilgrims to Fatima, that grace and peace may be abundant in all for deep knowledge of God and of Jesus Christ our Lord (cf. 2 Pt. 1:2). They will come to venerate the Mother of the Church, and, in the light of her luminous example and through her merits and intercession, they will go there to worship God, to offer Him expiation, to attract His mercy, and implore help and graces for the Church and mankind. I would like to share in some way and stimulate this aspiration that leads you to unite with Blessed Mary, the Mother of the true God and our Mother, and to trust in the motherly love she put in the mystery of redemption and in the life of the Church; the deep necessity of faith, hope and charity in the hour in which we are living, drives us to that.

For we actually find ourselves in an hour of radiant hope, in which the Church perceives that she is very close to man, really and deeply tied to mankind and to its history (cf. *Gaudium et spes*, no. 1). But it is also an hour full of responsibility in which the Church herself feels with greater force that a deep bond with Christ the Redeemer of man is indispensable for her.

And then, "Brethren, what shall we do?" To this question, once asked of St. Peter, his humble successor replies with the same word: "Repent..." (Acts 2:38). And conversion—as we are well aware, it is at the center of the message of Fatima—is a continual commitment to seek and bear witness to "deep knowledge of God and of Jesus Christ our Lord," the way of eternal life (cf. Jn. 13:3), which necessarily passes through penitence (cf. Lk. 13:3) and through prayer (cf. Jn. 15:5), which is for the Church in our days more than a need, a categorical imperative.

For this reason, a "pilgrim" with the pilgrims to Fatima, I exhort you to pray to Mary, through Mary and with Mary, holy Mother of God and Mother of the Church and Our Lady Help of Christians, trusting in her fullness of grace, manifesting to her, filial love and sincere devotion based on a resolution of faithfulness to Christ, faithfulness to the Church, and faithfulness to men our brothers. And may it be our Lady, our protectress, who presents to God the supplications I call on you to make in union with Christ, "mediator between God and men" (1 Tim. 2:5):

—for harmony within our Holy Catholic Church, so that we may live and bear witness to the mystery of redemption before all those whom Christ embraced and embraces with inexhaustible love;

—for the sanctification of the whole People of God—sacred ministers, consecrated persons, families, youth, children—that there may be vocations for consecration to service of the kingdom and to the evangelical witness of charity;

—for peace, justice, and brotherhood among men and among peoples; for those who are homeless, or live without peace, without religious freedom, without love and without hope; above all, for the little ones in this "International Year of the Child";

—for one and all of the pilgrims gathered in this sanctuary, for their loved ones, for their land and their country; that the Lord may comfort, protect and bless all.

With these wishes and with my heart in prayer, in token of abundant grace and peace, I bless everyone in the name of the Father, and of the Son and of the Holy Spirit.

Also available from St. Paul Editions

All Generations Shall Call Me Blessed

Rosalie Marie Levy

48 beautiful full-color Madonnas by great art masters of various lands. This Marian treasury contains the rosary, devotion of the Five First Saturdays, invocations, powerful novenas for all necessities.
131 pages

— MA0010

Cause of Our Joy

Sr. M. Francis LeBlanc, O.Carm.

A brief life of Mary and historical accounts of eleven miracles that have inspired so much profound devotion. Included—Our Lady of Fatima, Our Lady of Perpetual Help, Our Lady of LaSalette and the story of the Miraculous Medal. 174 pages
— MA0020

Glories and Virtues of Mary

Rev. James Alberione, SSP, STD

A moving presentation of Mary's heroic virtues and great privileges, drawn from Sacred Scripture and the Fathers of the Church. 251 pages

— MA0030

Hail Holy Queen

Rev. John H. Collins, SJ

Moving reflections on this prayer to our Lady. Full-color illustrations. 80 pages

— MA0040

Mary, Hope of the World

Rev. James Alberione, SSP, STD

A brilliant consideration of Mary under these aspects: in the mind of God, prophecies, and the longing of humanity; in her earthly life as Co-redemptrix of mankind; in her life of glory in heaven, in the Church and in the heart of the faithful. 222 pages

— MA0060

Mary, Mother and Model

Rev. James Alberione, SSP, STD

The history and aim of 30 Marian feasts, their part in the Breviary, and the benefits to be derived from their observance. Illustrated. 237 pages

— MA0070

Mary of Nazareth

Igino Giordani

In *Mary of Nazareth* we follow God's spotless Mother from the moment she received the Archangel's tremendous message at Nazareth, to the moment of her bodily passage into glory. Thereafter we follow her through history and see her grow in the love of men. Beautifully illustrated with three sections of Madonna art pieces by Panigati and Nagni. 182 pages

— MA0080

Mary, Queen of Apostles

Rev. James Alberione, SSP, STD

On Mary's mission of giving Jesus to the world. Superb approach to the imitation of Mary in the apostolates of desires, prayer, example, suffering and action. 348 pages

— MA0090

Mary "The Servant of the Lord"

M. Miguens, O.F.M.

An ecumenical effort is behind this scriptural approach to the Blessed Mother. The writer's purpose is to analyze the biblical statements about Mary and to place them in the appropriate scriptural setting. Mary is described in terms of all those "servants" of the Lord down the ages through whose agency God gradually and firmly carried out and continued His saving design. 198 pages

— MA0095

Mary, Star of the Sea

Rev. Albert Barbieri, SSP

"St. Bernard's famous words concerning Mary, Star of the Sea, form the subject of these thirty-one lofty meditations on Marian instructions, illustrated by appropriate examples." Rev. Gabriel M. Roschini, OSM 250 pages

— MA0100

Our Lady Among Us

Rev. Valentino Del Mazza, S.D.B.

Marian devotion grows through a deeper understanding of her role in salvation history. Her titles, her position in the Church, her privileges, virtues, glories and apostolates are the framework of this magnificent portrait of Mary who always lives among us. 169 pages

— MA0110

Ten Series of Meditations on the Mysteries of the Rosary

Rev. John Ferraro

Practical reflections compiled into ten series, making it possible to meditate points during each Hail Mary. Renders the recitation of the rosary more profound and fruitful. 232 pages

— MA0120

Daughters of St. Paul

MASSACHUSETTS
50 St. Paul's Ave., Jamaica Plain, Boston, MA 02130; **617-522-8911.**
172 Tremont Street, Boston, MA 02111; **617-426-5464; 617-426-4230.**

NEW YORK
78 Fort Place, Staten Island, NY 10301; **718-447-5071; 718-447-5086.**
59 East 43rd Street, New York, NY 10017; **212-986-7580.**
625 East 187th Street, Bronx, NY 10458; **212-584-0440.**
525 Main Street, Buffalo, NY 14203; **716-847-6044.**

NEW JERSEY
Hudson Mall—Route 440 and Communipaw Ave.,
Jersey City, NJ 07304; **201-433-7740.**

CONNECTICUT
202 Fairfield Ave., Bridgeport, CT 06604; **203-335-9913.**

OHIO
2105 Ontario Street (at Prospect Ave.), Cleveland, OH 44115;
216-621-9427.
616 Walnut Street, Cincinnati, OH 45202; **513-421-5733; 513-721-5059.**

PENNSYLVANIA
1719 Chestnut Street, Philadelphia, PA 19103; **215-568-2638.**

VIRGINIA
1025 King Street, Alexandria, VA 22314; **703-683-1741; 703-549-3806.**

SOUTH CAROLINA
243 King Street, Charleston, SC 29401; **803-577-0175.**

FLORIDA
2700 Biscayne Blvd., Miami, FL 33137; **305-573-1618; 305-573-1624.**

LOUISIANA
4403 Veterans Memorial Blvd., Metairie, LA 70006; **504-887-7631;
504-887-0113.**
423 Main Street, Baton Rouge, LA 70802; **504-343-4057; 504-381-9485.**

MISSOURI
1001 Pine Street (at North 10th), St. Louis, MO 63101; **314-621-0346;
314-231-1034.**

ILLINOIS
172 North Michigan Ave., Chicago, IL 60601; **312-346-4228; 312-346-3240.**

TEXAS
114 Main Plaza, San Antonio, TX 78205; **512-224-8101; 512-224-0938.**

CALIFORNIA
1570 Fifth Ave. (at Cedar St.), San Diego, CA 92101; **619-232-1442.**
46 Geary Street, San Francisco, CA 94108; **415-781-5180.**

WASHINGTON
2301 Second Ave., Seattle, WA 98121; **206-441-3300**

HAWAII
1143 Bishop Street, Honolulu, HI 96813; **808-521-2731.**

ALASKA
750 West 5th Ave., Anchorage, AK 99501; **907-272-8183.**

CANADA
3022 Dufferin Street, Toronto 395, Ontario, Canada.